One Man in His Time

A teacher, a method, and a madness

By

Dan Powell

authorHOUSE™

1663 LIBERTY DRIVE, SUITE 200
BLOOMINGTON, INDIANA 47403
(800) 839-8640
WWW.AUTHORHOUSE.COM

First published by AuthorHouse 04/22/05

ISBN: 1-4208-1408-7 (sc)

Printed in the United States of America
Bloomington, Indiana

This book is printed on acid-free paper.

For Julie, Bailey, and Lincoln

Contents

Acknowledgments

There is no way for you to begin to know how amazing the people in my life are. I would first like to thank Pearl the Bookworm for giving up her life so my siblings and I could have ours. Also thanks go out to Bill and Kathy for trying to rescue me, and to all my teaching buddies who *knew* that I was on the line where something begins or ends and encouraged me anyway. Thank you.

A special thanks goes to Mr. Justh, a teacher and father-like figure who took me aside during my first year and told me that I was going to kill myself if I didn't learn real fast what needed to be ignored, and it turned out to be much, much more than I first thought. He also sat down with me at a Chinese restaurant once and listened to "my story from the cliff". He has absolutely no idea how profound that was for me.

A tremendous appreciation is saved for Laurie and Denis, and all the others who welcomed me "where the earth meets the sky". I would also like to recognize my daughter Bailey the Cursive Girl for supporting my efforts on this project, especially the unsolicited cheek kisses. Equal recognition goes to my son Lincoln for using the back of my head as a worthy target for suction-cup-tipped arrows while I wrote. (I love you both, but I can still smack me some biscuits!)

As thankful as I am to all these people, nobody is more appreciated than my bride, Julie. Why she didn't chop me up, burn me, and flush my ashes down the toilet, I will never know. If you've never met a goddess, I present to you Julie Powell.

"All the world's a stage, and all the men and women merely players. They have their exits and their entrances and one man in his time plays many parts..."

~William Shakespeare
1564~1616

Jack of All Asses

If you press your lips tightly against a door window, such as one that might look directly into a classroom as students sit, and then blow as hard as you can, your lips and mouth spread out marvelously and reveal the oral cavity in such a sweet, indignant scene. It looks like you're trying to sing in a one hundred and ten mile an hour wind. Or I've also heard that it looks like the inside of a horse's mouth. Of course the longer and harder the blow, the more one can exhibit. This is all hypothetical of course, and not something I recommend you do unless your personal dignity is as immune as mine. Whoopsie there, it almost sounds as if I'm the wretch who dreams this up! Heavens to Betsy, you don't want to be mistaking me for that jack ass, no sir.

It's actually a fun thing to do on another teacher's classroom door. But make sure it isn't a math teacher first. They won't get it. Actually, a number of teachers might not get it, but you certainly have less chance with a math teacher I can tell you that from the start. Margie Tibbits was the best. She taught language arts and social studies and she laughed so hard I thought she was going to have an aneurism. She was bent over at the waist with her hands on her knees and not breathing properly, but she was just catching her breath for the next explosion of the giggles.

It's a sad thing for a teacher to say that he enjoys making fun of himself for the sake of the other teachers more than he likes to teach students but it's true. I would never have lasted as long as I have if I didn't. But I have to be honest. If I hadn't spent so much time around the immaturity of middle school students I'm not sure I would have become immature enough myself to create these zany ideas that make adults laugh. It's scary when I wonder what I would have become if I had chosen to be an air traffic controller. "Hey Charlie, lookie what I can do with my nostrils on this radar screen!" Nonetheless, I discovered I can make some people laugh with an adult twist on adolescent humor. Not really meaning to, but expressing myself helps me survive.

I heard an interview with someone one time. He was an integral and persuasive pillar of our civilization. One, without whom, our culture couldn't progress, and who possessed other qualities that pretty much eliminates us teachers as being even remotely critical to society. He was a professional athlete. But forget that for a moment, or longer if you wish. He told the interviewer that his number one priority in his working day was to make himself happy first, and everything else that matters took care of itself from there. I understand this because I think this is what I am doing. Actually, I don't know for sure what I'm doing. I think I'm just operating on instinct and there has been very little thought into the matter.

I read somewhere that when a person is crawling along in the desert, desperate for water, that the brain becomes aware of the danger and it begins to suck water up from the body to protect itself. It is going to make darn sure that it is the last thing to go. It is a beautiful defense mechanism. This is similar to how I survive my day at school except that preserving my brain has nothing to do with it, although it should. In fact, preserving my sanity has nothing to do with it either. You'd think that anything I would do out of self-preservation would defend at least some of my sanity. One would think that the total opposite would be true for teachers but it's not with me. I don't mind living on the edge of educational sanity for some reason. Maybe it's because that in the end, I know I don't matter. At least as a school teacher.

This is another way to make teachers gasp. I tell them that in the end that I don't matter, especially as a middle school teacher. Now understand, I am only speaking for myself. I'm not as business-like as many other teachers come across. It's too painful. I feel like I'm living in a world of make believe when I try to act like I really know what the hell is going on around me, and why we do the things we do. Pushing a kid right on to fifth grade when he still hasn't learned to read jumps to mind as one of the strange ideas we seem to just love. See, right now my dog is staring at me wondering why I gave the cat milk when I sure as heck would never do that for her. I would meet with more success explaining this to my dog than explaining to a decent, hard-working taxpayer why we tell kids they are doing great in school when they can't read.

I read a study one time that after kids graduate high school and became adults, they tended to remember their early elementary school teachers, and some of their high school teachers. A teacher the other day just told me she didn't remember any of her teachers. (How about that for all you aspiring teachers out there!) The middle and junior high teachers are left out in the ether. Which is okay with me because that's where I spend most of my day anyway. This is probably because during the middle years kids' brains are ticketed and towed because they are left unattended. Oh sure, there are a kazillion teachers who say that middle school students are best poised to learn of them all. This is a bunch of horsefeathers. Anybody with their brain tied behind their back can tell you this is simply not true.

This isn't to say, however, that these students can't be fun. Which is why it's easy for a guy like me to make them laugh. I know how to take them by surprise and never let them get used to me. One day I'm doing a soliloquy from *Love's Labour's Lost,* and the next day I have a pair of oversized eyeballs that I made out of half cut ping pong balls stuck in my sockets while a pair of OSHA inspectors come through my room. They're looking for things like overhead projector cords strategically placed across the floor that they could trip over, or emergency shut off valves for the flammable gas and so forth. They're not even aware of the absurdities lurking behind the half cut ping pong balls. I'm sure that activity like this is responsible for the water getting sucked up to my brain everyday.

Kids really like fart noises. I guess they're fun, what can you say? So it's not uncommon for me to be walking down the hall passing some kids on the floor working on a project while I cup my right hand around my mouth, stick my tongue out, bite down gently and give it a good push of air right from the diaphragm. If it's my first year in a school, it really startles the little things but not one month later when I do it, they say "Hi, Mr. Powell" without even looking to see who did it. There is something about my immaturity that really maximizes their readiness to learn, you know? Of course, educational research doesn't corroborate this but only because it is a new strand of research that needs

4

further exploration: Teacher Immaturity Coefficient and Student Achievement. No research is necessary for me, however. I know that fart noises put them at ease and raise their alertness.

I can't believe I'm even going to describe for you this next sequence. It's the sneezing snot/window cleaner effect I do on the overhead projector glass. By the way, the overhead projector is the greatest teaching tool of all time. The day they ban these from the classroom is the day I die as a teacher, if I'm not smacked out for some other reason first. I shouldn't even tell you this because I'm thinking about establishing this sight gag as a trademark. Anyway, if you do it, just give me credit for it. Here's how it goes. In a darkened room with no lights on except your overhead projector, grab your bottle of window cleaner when you're ready to erase the shark fin you drew, along with the shark you attached to it after solving for the hypotenuse using the Pythagorean Theorem. Any math teacher worth his salt will know what I'm talking about. Notice I didn't say the hypotenuse of a right triangle, because that would be redundant for a math teacher?

Okay, at this point talk like your very congested, act like you must sneeze and facilitate this by staring into the projector light. Squint with your eyes while you do this. Then with the diaphragm, project out a loud groan while simultaneously curling your lips and discharge a "sneeze" toward the glass on the overhead. Snap your head downward toward the glass and simultaneously give the spray bottle, conveniently hidden in the dark, a giant burst with your first and middle fingers. Make sure it is aimed at the glass. This will make even the kids with the worst attitude laugh so hard that they fart, because they think you actually blew some snot all over the projector glass and it's up on the screen for everyone to see. It's especially effective if you used green ink to solve your math problem, if you know what I mean.

You can also do a loogey version of this if you change the setting on the nozzle from "spray" to "stream", but you have to have a good sound effect for spitting for this one to work. Frankly, I'm beginning to think I'm the only math teacher in the country who knows how to do this. But there must be others out there. And this also works well on classroom door windows. This one made Margie Tibbits laugh so hard I had to go in and check on her. I loved Margie. I could try anything out on her. She had been teaching for many years so she knew to take it easy. She wasn't one of these overly serious new ones who would really prefer to throw a cot in the corner of their classroom so they could just live there.

I have this alter ego at my job. I ponder sometimes how it evolved and I can only come up with theories. No teacher I ever talk to believes that I wasn't always like this. I don't even know where the signs began emerging. All I know is that it happened. And like a seasoned actor who "drops" into character before every performance, I slip into my costume every day before I begin.

I usually wear black jeans and a white shirt and tie. This is my basic costume. The black jeans serve as a tough outer veneer. Many people think that teaching is a softy job but they are clueless. It is rough and ugly. It involves spills, stains and paper cuts. Sweat, abrasions, cramps and smelly socks. I used to change my socks at noon every day during my first year of teaching, because it was the only way at the time that I knew how to make it to the end of the day. Now I am much more sophisticated. I know how to control the biofeedback I get from my body, and I can regulate my own pedantic perspiration. (Oh that's good. I said *pedantic* perspiration and I meant *pedicurist* perspiration. I think pedantic means characteristic of a formal uninspired teacher; that's a good one.) Anyway, the black denim jeans are a must.

The white shirt is essential because it will match almost any color tie, and as a middle school teacher, I have collected some interesting ones over the years. I almost always wear a tie. Somehow the kids notice and they treat me like a dirt bag if it's not on. With it on, they only treat me like a dirt bag divided by four. It is an essential piece of my costume not only because of this, but also because I am convinced that it makes me smarter.

Every once in awhile, when I'm feeling overly confident, I try to convince my wife that I am razor sharp at school. That there are certain times of the day when it is virtually impossible to get the better of me. I can't think of any kid who can outwit me. They simply cannot get the verbal advantage over me. I realize that claiming superiority over eleven to fourteen year-olds shouldn't be something an adult boasts about, and it is generally true. But those who don't understand this advantage of mine simply do not have the experience of being in the salt mines with these darlings day after day, week after week, and month after month. There is no possible way they will come to appreciate this unless they have some sense of this. And frankly, just being the parent of one of these specimens doesn't always qualify their awareness. No sir, kids are like chlorine gas: they are more toxic the more concentrated they are. They morph into social insects, like on an ant hill, or hungry mosquitoes around a porch light.

So I wear a tie. And on the outside I look like an insurance salesman. Until I put on my last costume piece. My tool belt. That's right. Several years ago, I was driving to work and I was waiting at a traffic light near the construction site

7

Dan Powell

of a new Home Depot. It was the middle of winter and one of the crew walked around with his tool belt bouncing around his hips. I said to myself that those were the tools of his trade, and it started me wondering like many things do. What are the tools of my trade, I asked. And over the course of a few weeks, I put together a list of things that I use everyday to make myself more effective. I took this list with me to a pawn shop and found my own leather tool belt with three big bags slipped over it. In it I keep pens, pencils, calculators (scientific and graphing), a dictionary, a fly swatter I use for a pointer, a stapler, extra staples, rubber bands, paper clips, the *Essential Book of Facts*, a first aid kit, and a barf bag a science teacher gave me as a gift. I also have candy, a reference guide to the complete works of William Shakespeare, blank cards, scissors, overhead pens, dry erase markers, pliers and wire cutters for adjusting kids' braces, and a button with a picture of my mother on it, among many other items. Over the years I have collected gifts from others including dangling keychain dolls, and one of my favorites, a sideways view scope my sister-in-law gave me for Christmas. This one is fantastic for looking around my classroom door down the hall while students are in transition. I also have *Cultural Literacy: A guide to what every American needs to know*, along with a blow-up flying saucer that a student picked up at a Burger King when she went to lunch with her mom one day. She gave it to me as a gift. I used it for a remote hall pass. When kids ask what it is I tell them that it's my car. They look at me quizzically and I respond, "Well how else do you expect me to get to work from so far away?" They leave me alone for the longest time afterward.

Adults are the worst people to try to explain my tool belt to. They just don't get it. Math teachers tend to look

8

the other way when they see it for the first time. I don't feel obligated to explain it to them anyway. But kids can catch on almost immediately, at least seventh and eighth graders do. I spend so much time on my feet that I figured I was wasting a tremendous amount of energy walking back and forth to my desk for things I could have instantly, and believe me, I use everything in it. "Mr. Powell, what does *dolt* mean?" I hand him my dictionary. "Mr. Powell, can you staple this?" I pull out the stapler. "May I please borrow a pencil your highness?" I pull out the worst one in my bundle of one hundred plus, and give it to him. "Thank you my liege."

One time I had this kid who came into class after lunch greener than Kermit the Frog. His name was Bryan and he was a kid you'd all want your daughter to bring home some day. No really, he was smart *and* moral. After about ten minutes of graphing equations, he lurched forward and chucked up on the floor with the intensity of lightning. The rest of the class was so mortified that all they could do was slam desks outward radially leaving Bryan in the middle of the room like Alcatraz in the San Francisco Bay. They were dead silent. One more eruption from Bryan and half of them ran like people out of a burning building. I found out later they ended up in the library. Bryan's third toss was mostly air, but it still had some mass to it. Apparently marshmallows are seventy percent air, and they occupy some space yet, and so it was with his last blow. A few more kids left, but there were some like me who remained for the novelty of it I guess.

So Bryan catches his breath and props himself up to a slouch and manages to gasp at me, "Mr. Powell, I think I'm gonna be sick." (Oh great Bryan, let me know if you decide to.) And I pulled out my rubber gloves for the protective barrier just because I had them in my tool belt with the first aid kit. No way in hell was I going near Bryan's spontaneous creation, but I validated the contents of my tool belt anyway. Except for the barf bag because I couldn't get that out in time. Believe me though, it wasn't anywhere near big enough anyway.

So here's this shirt and tie guy cavorting down the hall of your local middle school, with a tool belt banging on the side of his hips, packed with teaching paraphernalia and interesting reference guides, whistling "You Are My Sunshine". He sees a pencil on the floor. What? Are you kidding? He sees two hundred pencils on the floor, it's a middle school! And he adds them to his collection. Why do I do this to myself is what other teachers ask. Mr. Justh, a science teacher, worries my back might give me problems some day, but this idea of mine saves me countless trips back and forth across the room or the building, and the other teachers for once, are not as efficient as I. And my alter ego is a faster thinker because of it. Go figure.

I am constantly wondering what I do to earn my check every month. Don't get me wrong, it's exhausting. But I am assigned to teach kids and there doesn't seem to be much learning taking place. I spend my day managing behavior and chasing down paperwork. I am a clerk. I am a social worker and a poor one at that. I have been called a babysitter, and much of the time I feel like one. What is it that I do that remains with them? Oh yeah, yeah, I know the lines. We are *touching the future.* We *make a better tomorrow.* I can honestly say that I feel that the state superintendents could care less about all that. What gets me is that they have become so data driven that everything we do must be documented and supported by data. Everyone is a data hound. Studies show this and studies show that. What really kills me is that we teachers are supposed to be these well educated, rational, critically thinking beings and I have met maybe one teacher in my life besides myself that wonders who underwrites and finances all this data we all go stampeding toward, like it's the face of the Virgin Mary mysteriously appearing on the back of a street sign. As if the data is going to save us. Whenever I bring this question up at committee meetings they always look at me like I'm some ignoramus. Well, maybe I am. But if so, I am an ignoramus who wants to know exactly who else has a stake in these research results.

Besides, if these Captains of Education were so into the data, they'd find plenty that supports this *future* thing or the *better tomorrow* deal. It must be out there, why don't they shove that in front of our faces? Everything is doubletalk, insanity and upside down. But my alter ego knows this and this is why I play the part of the guy hanging on the cliff. It's how I cope.

So instead of throwing myself into some new research-based strategy financed by some elitist special interest group, I practice chimpanzee noises outside my classroom door when I think no one else is looking, only to find Shelley Moffit, language arts teacher extraordinaire, looking at me like she just missed a chance to slip the straight jacket over my head. This is why I stand outside my door on "Open House" night whistling "If I Only Had a Brain" while parents come trickling into my room. You think I'm joking. My math students find me between classes standing in the hall, in a tool belt, performing Shakespeare monologues from *Henry V, Hamlet, As You Like It, Love's Labour's Lost, Romeo and Juliet,* and others. The kids walk down the hall and when they get to me their path bends completely to the other side of the hall like they were avoiding some crazed street person that their parents warned them about.

Maybe it's been a good thing that I never felt at least valued divided by two, because then I wouldn't have explored all these other paths. *Though it be madness, there is method in it.* If I believed in all the research, I never would've seen myself teaching math through *Hamlet.* Or perhaps it is *Hamlet* through math? I made sure that when my eighth graders were through with pre-algebra that they knew the entire story of *Hamlet.* This used to drive high school teachers nuts. "Don't do that," they would snap. "We get to that when they are seniors in high school!" The perfect time for teaching it, I think to myself. When their brains have dropped even further toward their feet. "You're not supposed to teach them English anyway, you're a math teacher."

It's disgusting. If they could have, they would have drinking fountains for the literature teachers, and other, skuzzier ones for the math teachers. Well, in my experience, I've found eighth graders to be the perfect age for *Hamlet.* They understand madness, probably because they see it in me all year. But they rivet themselves to me when I do some of the soliloquies. They know through me that Hamlet really did have a problem. I have Hamlet's "To be or not to be" monologue decoded for kids and prominently displayed around my classroom walls and they beg me to perform it, and they always applaud when I'm through. They don't do this because they think I'm Laurence Olivier. It's just that they understand something that many people tell them that they can't until maybe when they get to be a senior in high school, and their applause is really for themselves for getting it. That's how I see it anyway. Yeah, I know. I said they are not ready to learn and here I am telling you that they can understand Shakespeare. What should I do, commit suicide now?

Some of you are asking why. Why is he teaching Shakespeare in a math class? Well, the truth of the matter is there is math in *Hamlet*. Most English teachers won't see this, (actually, most math teachers won't see this either). Math is the language and science of patterns, and also in math we teach problem solving strategies. Among them are guess and check and eliminating possibilities. There are patterns in *Hamlet* too, and these two problem solving strategies are exactly what Hamlet uses to decide whether the ghost of his father is telling him the truth, and he does this through an ingenious test he puts his uncle through by having him watch "The Murder of Gonzago", a performance that some visiting players perform at Elsinore. In the play, Hamlet instructs the players to play out a scene that depicts exactly how his father was murdered according to the ghost. And when his uncle, the current king, becomes visibly startled when the scene arrives, this sets Hamlet into a vengeful, but in the end a tragic course of kick ass payback. Boom. Guess and check, and eliminating possibilities in action.

So Shakespeare ends up being a part of my student's schema after coursing through my classes. And it ends up being more than *Hamlet*. In the one hundred and fifty four sonnets he wrote, the Dark Lady appears more than a couple of times, there are patterns of immortality, and for some reason the word "stain" is repeated. What is up with that? Are not these mysterious patterns? It's the language first, then the plots, and then the characters that intrigue me in that order. The scholarly stuff I could care less about.

But what about factoring trinomials and solving inequalities? What about the meat of math that they're supposed to be getting from me? I can't answer that. I'm afraid that if I study it, they may actually know less after having me than before they arrived.

Every once in a great while, a parent would come to me concerned that his son or daughter was too distracting in class. This is by far not the norm. I maintain that often I am more distracting to myself than most kids could be. And this is because I am in a never ending search for self-stimuli. It's almost like I am autistic.

I am a singer. Well, actually my wife Julie is the singer. She's a gifted singer. But when you're married to a singer who is also a voice teacher, things rub off. One of the greatest things about teaching is that you have a built in captive audience that you can try things out in front of. One can invent things in the moment. So it happens during the course of my day when I can sing some old Frank Sinatra songs for the kids. They of course never heard of him, and this particular generation of kids I am confident will never hear of him. So where are they ever going to learn about Frank Sinatra and the math in Shakespeare if they don't hear it from me? It frightens me to entertain this thought.

Nothing of importance exists before the twenty first century to these kids. So they think I make up these songs on the spot. Sometimes, I do. I keep a piano in my classroom and make up songs about the kids as they come trickling into class, and when students come in tardy, I quickly changed to a minor key and sing improvised lyrics of disappointment and vengeance. Other songs I have invented were about myself as a teacher. "A Psychopath in Math" is a favorite among some of my kids, maybe because of the Gilbert and Sullivan style I give it. And one they don't hear so much is "Facedown On the Overhead". Whenever I sing that one they stand up on their chairs and hold up invisible lighters like they're at a Journey concert or something.

Other times, I use the music as a thinking strategy. Many math teachers suggest problem solving strategies like drawing a picture, creating a chart or table, or perhaps finding a pattern. I often have another suggestion. "Let's sing about this one", I'll shout. And I'll launch into what amounts to a musical think aloud about the circumstances at hand, what does the variable represent, what values do we know, why is the only Spanish in the textbook found only in the glossary, things of this nature.

"Where's the research on this, Powell?" some math teachers may snap. So I might respond, "Hey good idea. Maybe after you put your kids to sleep with your ball of fire lesson plan, you'll have a little time to do that for me." (Oh c'mon. I *never* talked to other teachers that way. Heh, heh.)

People who work with me know that I say crazy things out loud maybe for no other reason than because I like to hear how it sounds coming off my tongue. I am very peculiar about language in this way. Maybe this is what got me hooked on Shakespeare. Middle school students know I will say the nuttiest things in the nuttiest ways. They somehow know that I am experimenting. I am workshopping my ideas in front of them, seeing what works. The problem is I'm not sure what I'm creating all this for. Most of it leads nowhere, and of course I'm sure it doesn't help raise standardized test scores. I'm surprised I haven't been run out of town. Just to rile up the other teachers and get them thinking, I once wrote in my own writing, *...and then sniff,* under a box in the staff room marked "Scratch Paper". I also tried to start an anonymous poetry posting in the men's bathroom right above the urinal that I called "The Eternal Urinal", and that went over like a caveman at a debutante social.

I used to know this math teacher who had her desks in rows. In all aspects of class she was highly organized, efficient and ready. She looked like Linda Blair in *The*

Exorcist. Wow, did she know how to stare down a kid. Everyone was afraid that if they got too close or looked too long, they would become possessed too. And even the loudest idiot king of the school would behave in her class. She simply didn't put up with any crap. I'm sure she thought I was certifiably insane. I would often walk back and forth through the hall by her room when I was on my prep period, often singing. Maybe something like "Home on the Range". The stapler from my toolbelt might be clacking back and forth. I would glance in and see a student or two smile at me, and quickly look back at the board before they were caught looking out the door. Sometimes I would wonder how this teacher survived, working so hard and expending so much energy in creating silent, unhappy kids. But after years of the freak show that I produce in my room, I can honestly ask why I wasn't more like her. I wonder how many hours I have stolen from my students with my stupid songs and my sight gags. Could I have spent a lot less time on the life and times of William Shakespeare and taught more math? Although I think I taught all the math. Did I really have to show them how to make primitive- man teeth out of an orange peel? Is it possible that I am not necessary? Maybe this other math teacher went home with more energy. Maybe she was the one surviving, or even prospering by taking more of herself home after work each day. Maybe I really am the jack of all asses.

There are easier ways to teach. Unfortunately, I haven't figured out exactly how to do that yet. One would think that after ten years of doing this that if I haven't figured it out by now, then I'm not real quick on the uptake. Teaching is a giving profession. All I ever do is give, give, give. I don't have a plan for keeping my own cup filled because there never seems to be enough time. When I was in school I had a wonderful math teacher. She spoke several languages and sang arias. I think she eventually ended up having a nervous breakdown and getting divorced from her husband, also a teacher.

One day late in the week, on the way back from a weekly bus trip, I was sitting in a catatonic stupor. I know this is what I was doing because I was sitting right behind the driver looking at the slobber dripping off the corner of my mouth in the big mirror above his head. I was absolutely spent that week, and it was only a Thursday. I had thrown my pearls to the kids and had nothing left, not even for my own kids. I was literally falling asleep, which is a near impossibility on a full school bus. The kid sitting next to me, bored with his friend, turned to me and gave my shoulder a slight shove with his hand and said, "Hey, be funny." I don't remember having the energy to respond to him the way the situation called for because he was very demanding. But I do remember thinking that that's all I am to these kids: a child's plaything. I drove home that night thinking that this must be what a prostitute thinks, and it was about this time also that my six year-old son told me that he wished I wasn't a teacher anymore.

The Tragedian Begins His Show

I'll try and settle down in a minute. Right now, I can't.
Derek farted.

In class.

Again.

On purpose. And his mom is wondering what we
are doing to him here that is provoking him into such a
condition. I could never understand mothers like his. What
do you mean what are *we* doing to him? Are you out of your
mind? The kid is a seventh grader who would fit right in to
a kindergarten class, that's how mature he was. No middle
school kid intentionally rips up more wind than the month of
March right in class, and likes all the negative attention that
goes with it. What are *we* doing to him, give me a break!
This is what it all has come to. I'm trying to remember what
it was that compelled me to become a "teacher" and at this
moment, like all the others, I seem to be drawing a blank. A
very imposing blank that has utterly lost me.

I come from a middle school and teaching in one for ten
years has reduced me to this base, ignoble state. Somehow,
I have become this gigantic jack ass and I don't know

how it happened. I don't know what it was about middle school that contributed to my condition, but I wasn't quite the jack ass before I went into the business. I think what happened is that I sensed in my first week on the job that I was going to have to develop this cartoon-like alter ego as a defense mechanism. And over the years it has shot me through the roof of my pre-supposed limits of self-decorum and given me, among other side effects stomach pains, gas and now I'm thinking maybe hemorrhoids. And my gas thing you might think would give me a little more patience with Derek, except that, it doesn't. Nothing gives me more patience with him. No really, I wasn't the jack ass going in to this business.

I'm still trying to convince my wife Julie that when I was in high school I was the most on-the-ball person she'd ever hope to meet. But she doesn't believe me. I tried to tell her that Mr. Goldberg gave me a biology award when I was a sophomore in high school. He called me "the man with all the questions". But my wife dismisses that too, probably because I earned a D in biology in college and I had a bad attitude. Although I *think* my mom used to call me the jack of all asses; I don't know, maybe I just remember things differently

But Mom didn't know any better. She didn't know that I was headed for big things. I was driven that's for sure. I was headed for a good education. Inside my mind was flowing with ideals of nationalism, and pride, and the grand designs and God's plan for me, and the desire I had to blossom out of it all into meaningful contribution and prosperity. A real Abraham Maslow poster child. And I ended up teaching middle school. "Ahhhhng! Mr. Powell, Derek farted!" Absolutely delightful, just delightful.

No, I guess my mom did call me the jack of all asses once or twice, but like I said, I don't think she knew any better. She grew up in relative poverty as the eldest of many children, alcoholic parents, and the whole deal. She loved to learn, loved especially to read but as a young girl who wasn't taught to take care of herself in terms of hygiene, she quickly drew the wrong kind of attention at school and elicited some very serious abuse from the other kids. Very abusive comments. If I could go back in time, I would travel back to where I imagine she used to hide, perhaps in some out of the way alcove, sit with her and hold her close. I would promise this little girl that there is a tremendous world of compassion and beauty out there that she is destined to meet. That if she could just hang on, she'd find it soon. She's probably the reason I went into teaching in the first place, in some private, subconscious way. Only a dolt dreams all day long as a kid wishing to hear, "Derek farted!" *Wow, I think I'll be a teacher.* It defies the natural scope of things. Anyway, Mom dropped out of school before she could finish because she was encouraged to by the adults in her life including some teachers. She was living mostly with her grandparents, who I am told, loved her dearly. Her mother and father were three sheets to the wind most of the time and probably never had any grasp at all on the family thing.

So my mom became a survivor, and the concept of actually reaching self-actualization was an almost utterly alien concept to someone in this condition, although I knew she eventually read about self-actualization one day. Wow, she was a reader. It was her escape, but she was too "smart" to think it would lead her out of the trap. And so she didn't let it. So on the day she found out that I wanted to go to the U.S. Air Force Academy, I think she pretended that she was hearing something. She either changed the subject quickly, or I was actually being the jack ass she claimed I was and I was behaving in a way that actually required her to say something else to the effect of "tie your shoes," or "xyz," or something. I don't know.

I do know that she knew something about the Academy because I sensed she knew that achieving in school had to be a large part of it. She didn't want us to achieve in school. That is my belief. Isn't that a horrible thing for me to say? Maybe it's not that she didn't want us to achieve but it came across to me that she really didn't care either way. Nobody encouraged her to achieve; it wasn't part of her schema. I don't ever remember any messages about grades in school, just strong messages about behavior. She certainly didn't purposefully discourage us, and she would never hold that belief in an abusive way. Please, do not misunderstand this. But I think she wanted to protect us kids by not overtly believing in big dreams. She didn't want to see hopes and desires gunned down by the coldness of the circumstances of life. But the desire of youth gets whipped up, and not even a mother's sensibilities will stand in the way.

People say to me all the time, "How is it that you know so much Shakespeare, I thought you were a math teacher?" It is an odd combination I suppose, but one for which I haven't apologized. English teachers look at me like I have a third eye, and math teachers, in all their creative barrenness just have a difficult time taking hold of my style in the classroom. And I tell them, it is probably derived out of the way I grew up. I had a natural tendency for books and words, given to me by my mother no doubt, although I studied math every year in school. The math minor in college came about mostly by providential direction. Either that or it was a huge mistake, or something.

My siblings and I preferred to spend time with my mother who was infinitely interesting. We lived in this town that you might say was artsy and commune-like. Oh heavens, it wasn't commune-like, but it wasn't crawling with conservatives or capitalists either. Not that I remember. My Idaho home town was sprinkled with pot smoking "artists" who skipped up and down the roads barefoot singing to the trees. I don't think they wore any underwear either.

My mother would take us to these "openings" of some obscure European sculptor, who probably came to the U.S. because nobody liked their crap over there, and she would walk us around these horrible sticks of plaster with a little paint thrown on them, and try to explain to us what the artist was thinking when he made it. I surmised that he was drunk when it happened, and upon sobering up, still was equally uninformed about how it came to be. But what were we going to do? After inspecting these...I don't even know what to call them, they looked like airplane wreckage to me... after inspecting them from one side, she would walk us around to the other side ninety degrees and start over. Well this went on for five hundred and forty degrees or so, and then we went on to the next plane wreck.

These types of outings occurred from time to time over the years, and they must have had some cumulative effect on the mind of little Danny Powell, because when I got into high school, I had this fertile mind ready for learning difficult-to-understand concepts. None of this, "Where are we ever going to use this?" You hear kids blurt this one out? "Where are we ever going to use this?" Probably just parroting the corrosive idiots in the media they're all so entranced with. I always thought that was stupid of them to say when thirty minutes later they were down in the gym doing sit-ups. Where the hell do you ever do sit-ups in real life? Yes, I know you do them to help stay in shape, that's my point. But when we factor trinomials in math that's not contributing to mental shape? It's ninth century torture worthy of class action law suits. Makes me sick to even think about it.

Anyway, wondering where I was ever going to "use" something was a thought that never once crossed my mind because number one, every class I took, and every word I read, and every problem I tackled, was serving the purpose of putting me that much closer to the Academy. The purpose of it was well defined. I was too focused. Number two, and more dominantly I suppose, I enjoyed learning new things, whether they were abstract or not. And thirdly, probably most importantly, I was trained to try to make meaning out of anything that was put in front of me. Yet, I am rendered speechless when I hear, "Derek farted!" screamed out twice a day, often more. I can't handle that. Go figure that one out.

By the way, I did make it to the Air Force Academy. I was a proud young man. My mom didn't believe that it happened. She actually told me she thought it was a shot in the dark. Of course in my mind, it wasn't a surprise at all. It was just a matter of setting a goal and believing it would come about as the result of a lot of focus and hard work and visualization, belief, and faith. I went to bed every night with "USAFA or Bust" scrawled in crayon on the bottom of the bunk above my head, so it was the last thing I saw at night before I went to sleep, and the first thing I saw when I awoke in the morning. I used to imagine that I was already there when I drifted off, and when I woke up I immediately fed my mind the thought that I was there and had to get dressed and go run with the rest of the cadets. I believed I could do it long before I ever showed any potential. Strange, that belief often comes first. But, pure desire can do a lot for a kid. I didn't really know that my chances were slim. If I did, I didn't care. All I knew is that I was going to be one of them that went, and so I did.

Chapter one of the Success of Danny Powell, turned into one of the many chapters of The Failure of Danny Powell. I always thought it was ironic that one of the lowest points of my life was born out of one of my greatest accomplishments. A few short months after I had been at the Academy, I decided to leave. I quit. I somehow lost the confidence I had in myself. I had no more belief. I was surrounded by the most amazing people that one could hope to be surrounded by; they were special. I was part of a crowd of people that had high expectations of themselves. People who were there to help each other make it and I threw it all away. I remember an upperclassman that called me on the phone, I didn't even know him. He just identified himself as another guy from Idaho, and he told me not to get down on myself. This was before any thoughts of quitting entered my head. He told me not to do anything drastic without calling him first.

I met others like him. I could've *been* one just like him had I stayed. I quit. I'm convinced that's the worst failure of all. Especially this particular failure because I had everybody throwing me ropes and I chose not to respond. I let Senator McClure down, I let all the people at home down that supported me, and I let myself down...the most severe damage of all.

I had quit one time before. It was in sixth grade. I was racing during a P.E. activity that I was pretty good at. It was some sort of shuffle race, picking up erasers and moving them laterally between markers. No one had beaten me until I raced this one fifth grader. As soon as I noticed him ahead of me in our race, I stopped, and trotted real slow. I forgot all about that until I was sitting back home after quitting the U.S. Air Force Academy, wondering what I was going to do with my life. It was a very hard time for me, because I had no models. At the Academy, they were everywhere.

Quitting the Air Force Academy was an event that precipitated many years of drifting, and wasted youth. I was ashamed. Dejected and fossilized under several feet of hard rock guilt, I felt very unequipped and inexperienced regarding finding a way out. And waiting around to be "discovered" and slowly chiseled out did not appeal to me either. Maybe the worst part of it was the unspoken I-told-you-so, we're-not-cut-from-that-cloth look I got from my mom. She was affirmed…again.

So many phrases were derived out of situations like these: shoot yourself in the foot and dig your own grave come to mind. It was like Laertes in *Hamlet*, he ended up dying by the poison he put on his own sword. I could probably come up with some of my own if I tried. Locked myself out of my own car, or pulled the wrong tooth maybe. Julie came up with one several years later, although it didn't relate to my errors…I don't think. Sometimes she says, "I did a Lenny" referring to John Steinbeck's *Of Mice and Men* when Lenny accidentally killed his own pup. She says this when she's out weeding in the garden and inadvertently pulls up a flower.

I had once estimated that that one decision, to quit the Air Force Academy, had shaved eight to ten years of productivity from my life, perhaps more. I spent so long *not getting over it.* I had no idea at the time how that one decision was going to be the major defining moment in the life of Danny Powell. I am now almost forty one years old, and I still don't have the belief or the confidence that I had as that seventeen year old cadet. I have accomplished some things since then, but getting my confidence back isn't one of them. I have a master's degree, and two beautiful children. But I know my wife isn't as proud of me as she could have been. I wish she could've met the cadet, she deserves him. He was a kick. He wouldn't have disappointed her. She doesn't say it directly, but I know I disappoint her. I used to think that the perfect gift for Julie would be to erase all memory of me from her mind and slip in some other guy in her life who met her expectations a little better. Every once in awhile, I read about some elderly person that was interviewed and they lay this claim that they had no regrets in their life. Well, I have regrets of plenty of blunders against myself and others and I'm not even half way done yet. I hope I'm not half way done anyway.

After returning from the Academy, I tried going back to my high school. I talked with a couple of teachers, and I went in to see the principal, Mr. Lewis. I don't know what came out of my mouth but I distinctly remember Mr. Lewis saying that I didn't have to apologize. But I knew better, because they all supported me with great faith. Crap, that was a hard time for me.

Somehow, I was given some help though during this self-defeat. There was this man and his wife, Bill and Kathy Yost, who seemed to take a liking to me. They must have seen something in me that nobody else did. Bill was the only person in my existence who had the courage to tell me that I failed, but that there is always failure, and that I will know success if I could learn a couple of strategies. What the hell, nobody else was coming forward to help and I didn't know where to start, so I let them mentor me. The strangeness of this to me now is that Bill and Kathy were in their very early thirties at the time, but they seemed like aged sages to me. And when I became their same age, I wasn't a whole lot better off than I was when I was eighteen and trying to dig myself out of this mess. This is partly how I derived the ten year plus figure of my wasted life of productivity.

The Yost's had a resort on the lake where I grew up and they asked me if I would watch over their house and their cabins for the winter while they were away helping out Bill's brother. I was cognizant that they were a successful couple, because of their youth and enthusiasm, as well as their successful business. They left me a snow worthy vehicle and a freezer full of food, and every once in awhile, they sent a small amount of money. I guess they wanted me to spend the winter thinking about the mistake I made and form a strategy to get my life back on track. These people were royalty to me. It is crucial that this be known. I was in deep, deep need for mentoring and they appeared. I will always be thankful to them for their willingness to show me the way. They were a prince and a princess. Although this was thoughtful of them, I was either still immature or too stupid or both to accomplish what I thought they had in mind for me. They were wonderful and eventually pivotal people in my life even though my time with them was very, very short.

The next fall, right after I arrived at college and began piling up student loan debt for absolutely no direction or purpose, Bill and Kathy were killed in a horrible sail boat accident with two other couples. It involved a sudden, freak wind storm and electrocution when their mast struck a power line that spanned a small bay of water on the lake. The boat burned, and then as a brutal gesture of fate, they all drowned to boot. They left two very small children behind. I was devastated. The degree to which I mishandled this event emotionally, may have been what prevented me from a quicker recovery from failing myself at the Academy.

For two weeks I would often wake up in the middle of the night and not know where I was going to run and hide from my roommates in the dorm, because I didn't want them or anybody else to see me sobbing like a baby. It was like being sick, you know, sometimes you don't make it to the bathroom, and you have to do it right there. Luckily, this new roommate I met, Keith, would find me in the corner kneeling down weeping my eyes out while everyone else slept. They were probably drunk anyway. But Keith did nothing but place his hand on my shoulder and rub my neck and he would whisper affirmations to me and encourage me to breathe. He did this two or three times throughout two weeks. Keith recently had a close friend pass away, and because of this he probably somehow saved my life.

The worst part of this little episode was that it was the beginning of a long and agonizing era of college education for me. It was the beginning of me stuffing four years of college into seven. I knew all about the curricula of all the colleges because I was enrolled in all of them from one time or another. I was pathetic. Engineering, general studies (I do not recommend this one), music, industrial technology, math, and finally psychology. To be honest, there may have been another one in there somewhere. I was so sick of changing my mind and my idle indecisiveness I actually committed myself to finishing in psychology because I was tired of changing and tired of Prozac or whatever the hell it was. The degree in and of itself was damn near worthless Oh it gives me a rash to think of all the months and years I wasted, not to mention ten or more years of student loan payments ahead of me for a useless diploma. Yikes.

There was a very bright light of hope in the middle of all this when I visited a Marine Corps recruiter. He was impressed by my physical fitness scores and encouraged me to apply for the Platoon Leaders Course, an officer training program in Quantico, Virginia that led to flight school afterward. I could pick up where I left off at the Air Force Academy, and get my life back together! I was training everyday and motivated in my classes. I was called into the recruiter's office often to complete paperwork, tests and other administrative details and on one such occasion, I was informed that I was dropped from the program because of some medication I had been prescribed. The damn anti-depressants. I had either overlooked reporting these or I thought that it was like ibuprofen and that it didn't need reporting. Pow. Another shot in the jaw. It's funny that even then, at twenty one, I felt like my life was slipping away. After a few more years of waffling around, I met Julie and fell absolutely head over heals for her. And for some reason, when I asked her to marry me, she said yes and I forgot all about flying or anything else for that matter. It was a *tremendous* gesture of faith on her part.

We started out our marriage with our nine year-old ring bearer being clobbered to death by a drunk driver on his way home the night of our wedding. His entire family was with him and sustained serious injuries. But little Jacob didn't even have a chance. I was his Big Brother in the Big Brothers and Big Sisters program. I don't think he knew his father, who I think was in prison somewhere. Of course, the idiots driving the truck that hit them head-on at highway speed all walked away from the crash without so much as a limp. (Why does it seem to always happen this way?) This was a tough way to begin. Every time I see our wedding pictures I think of what that kid could've become had the beer-swilling co-eds not interfered and taken his life. Consequently, I have no patience whatsoever with people who think driving tipsy is socially accepted, or even comical. None.

Somewhere crammed in between my wedding and my first year and a half out of college with my degree in psychology "firmly" in hand, I established a life to be proud of. I managed to sneak in six weeks of failure in advertisement sales, followed by an equally successful six months of door-to-door insurance sales, a miserable showing of about a month of health insurance sales, and eight months of computer networking hardware sales, which ended with two choices served up to me by management: quit or be fired. Ever hear of a track record? I did learn something from all this, however. For example, while selling door-to-door, I learned to identify the size and breed of a dog looking only at fence height and food dish circumference. My wife however, was devastated. All joking aside. I remember her crying and telling me, "You ruined everything!" Who was I to deny it?

So there I was, ten years after my high school graduation and the Air Force Academy opportunity long since pissed away, unemployed in February with a hall of fame track record backed up by the most marvelous college degree one could imagine, deep in student loan debt, no prospects and a wife heartbroken at my ineptness. And it wouldn't be the only time I would leave her feeling this way. There were worse times to come. At the time we were living in rented lodgings with Julie's sister with everyone wondering how we were going to make it what with all my gifted decision making skills and all.

To be honest, I don't even know how I managed. Why wasn't I scooped off the planet? I think I took an acting job

31

because it had the potential of twenty eight cents a week or something pathetic like that. After that I worked in a campground checking people in who drove forty foot motor homes and who did the giant sunglasses deal and who wore the powder blue jumpsuits and belonged to Good Sam clubs. (I learned later from one of my principals that they wore these clothes to provide comfort for gas pains, or something like that.)

So somehow, after years of drifting, waffling, indecision, bad decision, and failure, I figure I was finally fit to become a teacher. So together with Julie, we decided I would go back to college and become certified to do so. One year of core courses and fifteen months of graduate school. The first year was me living away from Julie with my sister and brother-in-law, which was probably good for Julie because she needed some distance from me at this point. I always wondered if she was thinking about setting me on fire while I was sleeping or something like that that you might read about in an article tucked away in some small town newspaper. You know, the stories they feel obliged to mention but not to sensationalize because everybody knows the bastard deserved it anyway? Although we saw each other every weekend, I did miss her.

I really wanted to become an English teacher, but in the course of making myself marketable, I picked up a math minor, and ended up becoming a math teacher. Being an English teacher somehow seemed like this lofty ideal. A sage for the students to look up to and derive confidence from. One who would know about life's failures and passages. I'm glad I didn't become one because nothing could be further from the truth, especially since I still didn't feel qualified or even confident enough to teach English.

Besides, I would've ended up grading parent's papers, since they were the ones who wrote them anyway.

This, as it turned out was a favorable thing because I have come to love math as a philosophy, and a place to go to for the truth. At least I used to love math. As the years passed, this has become less the case and the liberal system has beaten out any shred of fascination I ever had for math in me in the first place. Actually, this is not quite true. I do enjoy it at home, privately in the late hours. Like whiskey, I suppose. My fascination with it grows back over the summer months. But to teach it in a public school has become a foul and loathsome assignment. Math has fell victim to moral relativism, and as such, it is deemed to have no more the correct answer than anything else.

This is of course absurd to those of us that know better. But to those who don't, i.e. many teachers and administrators, math is suddenly being transformed into a supposed amusement park ride, where if it isn't stomach-in-your-throat fun, then somebody's not teaching it correctly. Again, this is absurd to those of us that know better. I have been taught that if math is not difficult, learning is not taking place. I don't understand for the life of me why they don't want this to be true. The public wants learning to be this effortless, ethereal experience without a trace of adversity or discomfort on the part of the learner. In other words they want it to be like having a television on. Although having a television on for me is something different than being "effortless". Agonizing comes to mind. My mother Pearl the Bookworm used to threaten to chop the TV in two when we were kids. And my wife and I have not had television in sixteen years.

I used to speak up at conferences on assessment when the attendees were asked about the qualities of a good test.

Dan Powell

"When I have failed. Just as in life's tests. Those were always the ones where I learned the most", is usually what I would say. A gasp would blow across the room like I had just admitted guilt to a murder, and teachers would turn their heads to see what lost soul would say such a thing. Especially the women middle school and elementary teachers, who get the shivers when anyone utters the f-word of failure. I can't figure out where these people come from.

I remember being in a teacher training session with a TOSA (teacher on special assignment). I don't know exactly what we were discussing, but I do recall it was on the topic of assessment. She said, "Never tell them that they failed!" And then she shuddered, as if it was akin to having a drunken toothless, good ol' boy cozy up to her. I couldn't understand what was up with that. I've learned plenty from it. I guess she prefers to have a student's first exposure to failure of any kind occur after they are well out of the public school system. You know, by then they will be the least capable of dealing with it. This kills me. It's almost as if these people want to produce ineptness. (Although, in my own history, I certainly did a good job of this to myself on my very own.)

But the truth of the matter is if you don't know failure, then you can't know success. How are we supposed to tell them apart otherwise? Failure is going to happen to people in some flavor whether we trick them and force their heads in the sand or not. I just prefer to *teach* kids to recognize it and manage it as it comes along. Others wish them to be ignorant of it.

I happen to be intimately acquainted with failure, so where is my success?

I'm not sure but I think it has been that I figured something out. For me it came as a moving target. It was

34

like taking swings at mosquitoes, I was never going to land the death blow as long as it was darting back and forth in front of me or behind me for that matter. Isn't it much more effective and sane to wait for it to appear in the opportunity of stillness? Ralph Waldo Emerson wrote about the secret of nature being patience. I spent so many years looking at what other people deemed success and I saw that there was no hope that I had what it took to fit into their schemes or subcultures. You know, Amway or the country club crowd. And of course there are others. It couldn't have been spelled out better for me than Shel Silverstein did in *The Missing Piece*. The protagonist rolled along in an adventure looking for what it thought would be the fulfilling piece, meeting many possibilities and diversions along the way, not even noticing what was there when he was happiest. Go back and read *The Missing Piece,* and pay special attention to when the butterfly appears, and what returns when you think the story has ended. Or perhaps I learned my lesson from Dorothy in *The Wizard of Oz,* who exclaims at the end that if it can't be found in her own back yard then it was probably never there to begin with.

It reminds me somewhat of the problem solving my students did for so many years. Entry tasks aimed at the lateral thinking crowd were always a hit with some of my students. Often, I noticed that the solution to many of the problems were contained in the problem itself, right there underneath your nose. My students recognized my question, "You know how the answers can sometimes be found *right there?*" That's what made itself very obvious to me in *The Missing Piece.* It's funny that after reading so much English and American literature (I know, this makes me an ignorant, bold-faced bigot for reading all this white European trash), and all the success books, and the complete works of William Shakespeare, that I really found what I needed in a children's book. In a way, it's a testament to my oversight and somewhat embarrassing. But in my schema, it doesn't surprise me when I look back on it.

So what are our other missing pieces? What is it that we've always known? What are we learning? I had a counselor ask me this once, "What are you learning?" It's a great question because it's not as easy to answer as it seems. They seem so inert but indeed are very powerful questions. Just like the butterfly. Once you identify what it is that is important to you, for example your core beliefs and attitudes, then opportunities are more noticeable and available to you. The part of your brain that is ready to identify things that may be useful to you is called, I think, the reticular activating system. This I remember from my prized degree in psychology, and when this system is activated, you start making a difference. When the student is ready, the teacher appears.

I am, and always will be a student. My problem with these discoveries is that it took me many years of black eyes and bloody noses to even become smart enough to recognize them when they finally made themselves known to me. By that time, some may have considered I wasted half my life. For the most part it wasn't time well spent. I was the club treasurer of misspent youth, however, it was not entirely wasted either. Have you ever seen the bumper sticker, "All Who Wander Are Not Lost?" Well I believe that some are lost. I know I wandered and I was plenty lost. I've heard of lost hikers that panicked because of the unfamiliarity of their surroundings and were eventually found distraught and confused...very close to the trail.

I've dealt with many kids who were very close to the trail and parents as well. I'm convinced that the only thing consoling them at times was the sound of my voice affirming them that they weren't far away. Some of them heard something in me, as if I had passed through that land myself. They trusted me and I'm pleased with that. They heard the sound of a man who knew. And every once in awhile, in a big way, I wish I didn't.

The Economy of Movement

It was March 2 and the drive to work was actually not that uncommon. I normally look at other folks going to work. It's part of a game I play on my way to my work. I'm sitting at a stop light and I look around me, surveying the faces behind the wheel including the one behind me and I speculate what it is they do for a living, or where it is they are going if they look like they don't work. One morning I saw a woman in an early 1970s Ford LTD, you know, one of those cars that occupy about an acre of road space. The curlers and the bathrobe were too cliché, but together with the bumper sticker it was a hall of famer: Men Are Idiots And I Married Their King. Some days I imagine I see insurance salesmen making their way to a morning meeting. Others, I see real estate speculators or drywall hangers.

Another morning I was cruising down the freeway and I looked in my rear view mirror, and I saw this object approaching. It looked like one of those supersonic UAV recon drones used by the CIA, and it passed me like I was driving in the opposite direction. It was my neighbor, the dentist. He must've been late for a denture job, or something a little more profitable than a cleaning. At least I think it was him, the car was gray. Rather, the blur was gray and I thought I saw GR8TETH on a license plate. His car had been enveloped in that condensation vapor you see that surrounds the wings of jets. But I knew who that was and I know where he was going, so he doesn't really count. (But what does count is that he is a great neighbor and a tremendous dentist, especially good with kids!)

The people who pass me at a more reasonable speed are more interesting to take note of. You see, I drive just under the speed limit on the freeway because it helps me manage my space and following distance much better. I am not crowding anyone in front of me and the space behind usually stays clear as well. I can also maintain a 12 to 15 second visual lead time to help me make and execute decisions about what obstacles or road conflicts may be coming ahead. In addition, the extra space in front lets me target 20 seconds ahead on my path of travel. It's also a very philosophical way to drive. Sort of a Zen approach to traffic safety that relates, really, as much to life skills as it does to driving.

The point is, however, that because I drive just a bit under the traffic flow, it takes most traffic a little longer to pass me than it would otherwise. So I get a real good read on them when they pass. If they're slumped over I know they don't enjoy where they are going. If they're on the phone I know they never stop working and their kids are smart asses in school. When they smile I know they are on their way to the airport, early, to catch a flight to Fiji. And when they flip me off for not going the speed limit, I know they are teachers. And it's late in the school year, but it's still far enough from spring vacation that it's not reasonable for them to get hopes up too high. And it's probably early in the week which brings me back to March 2.

I know it was March 2 because it was Dr. Seuss's birthday. And incidentally, this particular year it was early in the week, a Tuesday. This day I was dressed as the Cat in the Hat. It really wasn't the big red bow tie that got me thinking about this. Nor was it the striped hat which was smashed down around my eyebrows by the car ceiling or the big black whiskers I drew on my face that stretched to my ear lobes and highlighted with my young daughter's temporary tattoo makeup. It was something else probably in the quizzical looks and the entranced stares of other drivers. Where on the planet, they thought, does that poor man work? I imagined that they had me as a book store cashier that day. Maybe I was mistaken for some sap who was evading a warrant for arrest. Or perhaps I framed houses and I just wanted to surprise the guys with my literary flair.

Not once did I suspect that I was ever taken to be a teacher. A middle school math teacher of all things. How the hell do math teachers ever have time in their hopeless devotion to lesson plans to portray some strange jack ass who shows up at the door of two unsupervised children? No "stranger danger" warnings or anything. Forget it. I'm not going to explain it to you because I can't. What do you want from me, answers? I don't have any, and I don't bring it up because I offer insight. I mention it because I have to. Maybe I'm not devoted enough to be a math teacher. It's all part of how I manage my confusion.

Math teachers are supposed to be these rare, organized individuals that can compute at lightning speed. They know exactly what page they are going to be on three months hence come hell or high water. Sitting at meetings with them is like being in a room full of statues. That's how much personality they have. They couldn't be drawn off the linear thinking path by an earthquake. Thinking outside the box for them is switching their seating chart from alphabetical order to reverse alphabetical order. So I'm not rare and I'm certainly not organized all the time. Am I supposed to slit my wrists now?

I watch these two painters pass me real slow on the freeway. The guy in the passenger seat is closest to me, of course, so he gets a real close look at the whisker thing I have going on. That and my nose is bright red and outlined in black and white. As they progress past me, suddenly they slow down ever so slightly to glide back even with me. Probably to get a second look or perhaps to let the driver have a look. Sure enough, the driver leans around. He has a cigarette bouncing up and down from his lips. He takes a peek at me and off they go again giving way to the Mary Kay distributor behind them taking her daughter to school, with the young girl's coat and part of her seat belt closed in the door and flapping in the wind. Somehow, they don't notice me. And this of course clears the way for the man listening to motivational tapes, who I can only assume, is an accountant, or another teacher. He sees me, stops the tape and wonders what to do next. I think he pretended that he didn't see me. Some people do that when they are out of their comfort zone. They come from the School of Look the Other Way, just like the schools run by the Politically Correct Administravia Protectorship. If one looks the other way, then somehow it makes it so what they saw isn't really happening.

This of course was only one of many mornings. Working in a middle school can have the boon of many interesting commutes. Halloween time, for instance, is usually one of the best. Not only is it possible to catch a glimpse of someone else sneaking to work in their costume, although that is very rare, it is a good opportunity to show off mine to the other commuters. One such late autumn I got the chance to smile at passersby and flash them my movie quality, custom fang tooth caps that accessorized my Dracula outfit.

As fun as that morning was, it didn't even compare to the year I put a giant white plastic sack around me, tied it up around my neck and called myself white trash. This was my brother Joe's idea. (Some people think *I* am clever and witty. I'm muscle bound between the ears compared to Joe. He has to be the quickest and most clever person I've ever met.) Anyway, and not surprisingly, it went over like a two story outhouse with the PC Administravia Protectorship, which you would think would allow a hyphenated Caucasian-American like me to have a little fun with it, I mean, I did live in a trailer once. But the Protectorship didn't let me. There was no fun to be made of people like Dan Powell that day, I tell you what. I thought for sure my hyphenated identity would appeal to some sensibilities, but it didn't. I guess it only works with liberals, blacks, Mexicans, recently re-married women, gays, Europeans, Hollywood actors, celebrity athletes, Asians, and certain hybrids of dogs. Being a white male, it was flat out condescending of me to even bring it up, I guess.

I had to change back in to something boring when I got to my classroom. I think it was something politically neutral like a pumpkin or something. Yes, one of the other teachers had an orange trash bag that I switched over to. Nonetheless it elicited some mighty frowns and concerns from my fellow commuters. Most of them looked at me with that someone-has-to-be-the-adult-around-here look on their faces. Bunch of pasty-faced stiffs, that's what I say, just like math teachers.

I always wonder if I am a familiar face to some of these people, and they have actually had the fortune to catch me on a couple of these occasions. I mean, I often see the same vehicles at about the same place on the interstate. Why wouldn't they recognize my car as well? They must wonder, too. I've driven to school in many costumes before, they must go home at night and tell their spouses something, maybe after the kids go to bed?

As I mentioned, most math teachers I knew weren't going to change their lesson plans even for the second coming of Christ. Even He was going to have to wait. Somehow, I slipped through the cracks of this thinking and was plucked from the crowd of these stiffs, although I don't know who plucked me. And I drive to work with other issues on the front and edges of my mind.

Some math teachers on their way home may estimate the standard deviation of a set of recent test data. I always find my mind slipping away to something else. I have worked at three different middle schools and the commute for each of them has been slightly longer than thirty minutes, a long half hour to a longer half hour. Quite a commute divided by two, you might say for the sake of the math stiffs. Time is less than or equal to thirty eight minutes. Yes, anyway, I cross a state line roughly halfway through, maybe closer to total distance times .57, is where the state line rests, or times .43 if you're traveling the other way. And one afternoon on the way home, I was contemplating a drawing one of my students was doing in an art class, which of course wouldn't be interesting to most math teachers I knew. Her teacher had her doing a self portrait of her dressed in a period costume.

Knowing this girl and her mother, I never thought that the daughter looked anything at all like the mother. Not remotely. And when kids draw, especially the ones that are not talented sketchers, the results don't always look like the subject. This was not necessarily the case with this student. What she was drawing looked quite nice actually, but it didn't entirely resemble her own face.

You're probably wondering at this point what I was doing in her art class when I had a class of my own right across the hall. Yes, well mind your own bees wax, I was curious. And besides, I was indeed just a couple of steps away. I studied what she had produced so far, and it wasn't until I looked at it upside down that I saw a striking image of her own mother on the tablet! This is where my mind slipped away to on this particular drive home.

I have always found the commute both ways to be a welcome and necessary part of my day. I give myself the opportunity to wind up, and to wind down. I think I was sipping on an ice cold Coca Cola. My mind had grabbed on to this drawing and it wouldn't let go. I had begun to wonder if this girl was replicating her own image, or perhaps sketching herself as she wished to be, which is a very viable thing to do not just as an artist, but as a kid dealing with the painful throbs of self-consciousness that accompany kids like her through adolescence.

This experience gave way to the concept of perception. Did she know that it looked like her mother? I didn't dare mention it to her lest she interpreted that negatively. I immediately mentioned it to her teacher, though. And on the way home it propelled me back to my early twenties when I read *Zen and the Art of Motorcycle Maintenance*. I remember there being a description of riding in a car being akin to watching television: looking through the windshield wasn't quite the authentic experience that riding on a motorcycle provides. (Of course, watching an inane television program isn't anywhere near an authentic experience. It is programmed by idiots, for idiots.) On a motorcycle one is experiencing the actual context of the scenery with few barriers to shield you from the *Truth,* as it might have been written about in *Zen.* Welcome to where thoughts can take a simpleton math teacher.

What is an absolute scream though is seeing students at a stop light near the school. They are in the passenger side of Mom and Dad's SUV and they are, for all intents and purposes, right next to you. No matter how big of a jerk a kid can be, they love seeing a teacher outside the walls of a school. Well, that's not entirely true.

Anyway, one morning this was the case. I arrived at the light first. I happened to be playing with this toy robotic-like arm that belonged to my nephew. (He left it in the car one day and I found myself playing with it to and from school for a couple of years.) I was squeezing the trigger on it and it makes the hand, or fingers rather, open and close. When this particular kid and his parent pulled up next to me, the kid about peed his pants because, you know, there was his dingbat math teacher sitting next to him. One could see that he started squealing with excitement to his dad, who didn't like me anyway. I guess I wasn't serious enough for him. He preferred something more like the plague in his son's math classroom that was for damn sure. Anyway, the robot hand incident happened a lot over the course of a couple of years and I didn't want to disappoint this youngster. I felt like the school year car pool Santee Claus.

So, I pull this toy arm and hand up to the window and wave to him by opening and closing the fingers. Then I thought, what the heck, he's a bright kid, he can handle something a little more challenging. So I start to mimic a little nose picking job that sent the kid into hysterical laughter. His dad glared at me like I just pulled a knife on him. Yes, yes, yes, I know, someone has to be the adult around here.

Traffic lights however are not always pleasant. Especially when in the car next to you sits a disgruntled, former student. You must understand that because I am more of a three dimensional cartoon in the class, some kids think, "Oh, he's lively and fun and energetic, so I must be able to do anything in class that I damn well please." This is their thinking. My teaching personality has given me so much grief because of this. This describes this next particular subject.

It had been three years or so since this kid was failing miserably in my class, and because of that, our third world public school system rewards him by sending him on to high school. And some people think I'm the lunatic. So I hear this honking next to me, and I know it's some delightful high school student next to me, so I refuse to look. The light doesn't change and the honking continues. So, I decide to error on the side of humanity, turn my head to look, perhaps expecting to see someone with a sign that says "Smile, God Loves You" or something else inspiring. Instead, I see what's his face in the passenger seat, at 7:15 in the a.m., a cigarette and a can of Pepsi in one hand, and nothing but a middle finger in the other. His face carried a loaded firearm of disdain. Absolutely delightful. At least he was up. Most high school students were still lying in their coffins avoiding the garlic cloves.

I knew that he lost his father long before he ever came to our school. He was a state trooper in Alaska and he was shot. It was heartbreaking at one time I'm sure. However, this was not the time to cast pity on him. The kid was an absolute jerk. I know what you're thinking. How could anyone who calls himself a teacher say that? It's easy, just try it. I can already hear the politically correct teachers gasp, which doesn't bother me any, it just tells me I'm on the right track.

There's a certain cast of female teachers that are somewhat difficult to describe. Most of the time they are elementary teachers, they're either unmarried and have been teaching for a month, or they are married to some highly successful professional, have been teaching for years and don't need the income. There's this subtext about them that expresses an overabundance of tolerance, and the they-are-just-kids attitude. Abundance is okay, an overabundance tends to get in people's way. There's nothing inherently wrong with them beyond this of course, but many times these people are simply not in touch, and consequently they miss the nitty gritty elements of certain issues. For example, they are not fond of acknowledging jerks as jerks. It's *always* masked by some other "disorder" that is miles out of the kid's control.

For instance, let's say that, hypothetically of course, nineteen Middle Eastern hijackers commandeered three jumbo jets and intentionally flew them and their innocent passengers into a fiery oblivion at three different locales, killing thousands of other innocent people. These particular teachers would say something like the hijackers weren't breast fed as babies or that they had teachers that lectured instead of using cooperative learning techniques, or something else even more absurd, somehow excusing their murderous actions. To say, in effect nothing about the completely innocent victims on the planes that had promising and fulfilling lives of their own. Sometimes, these teachers are utterly oblivious to this.

Well, I'm sick of being politically correct. One can't deny that the world is full of adult jerks, and these jerks were once little jerks. And the PC police say, "Well, his father was shot." Yes, I know that. Remember, I'm the one who told you. This is probably *why* he turned into a jerk, and he knew that the PC bleeding hearts would let him get away with anything. He learned early on that because his father was shot, and that his math teacher seemed like a jovial entertainer, he could legally do anything he wanted. He remains a jerk however, although he possesses the ability to change. Besides, I've met other kids who lost a parent, and they did not turn into jerks.

Driving home is a blessing. It gives me a chance to breathe and put some distance between me and these types. They are certainly not prevalent in the middle schools I've been in at least. Right before I cross the state line I see this sea of Idaho mountains with open arms, telling me how much they missed me. All the futile efforts I made pissing in the wind in a public school don't matter to them. They let me in anyway. It's almost like they know I'm in a battle I can't win, that I'm the only conservative teacher in the multi-million militant membership of the teacher fraternity. Yeah, yeah, yeah, I know, no conservative teacher dresses like the Cat in the Hat. That's part of the insanity of Mr. Powell. Nobody can quite figure him out. But the Idaho mountains understand me. They are like my dogs at home except the mountains don't do disgusting things in the backyard when guests are over. Or even when guests aren't over.

It doesn't matter what happened during the day at school. When I cross the state line on my way home, I sense this physiological change. A load drops and I feel free again. When I teach school, I show up in the morning in this trap. Like the roach motel…you check in, but you don't check out. No matter how hard I try to maintain perspective, and to remember there is a big picture and more important things waiting for me on the outside, my life is not my own as soon as I get in the school building. It's like I become temporarily brain scrubbed and I forget who I am, and all about my worth. I become this cog in an ineffective wheel, unaware that I even exist. I forget that I am an integrated human being and I'm hooked up to a life-sucking machine. Only when I break out of the doors and run for my car, fighting the urge to look back, and I begin to drive away does any hope reassert itself on my consciousness. I become me again. What is a man doing to himself when he is aware of this?

I was caught in a wolfpack of traffic one day on my way home. There was some incident on the freeway that compromised traffic flow, perhaps an injury accident, or a man leaning on a shovel or something. Whatever it was it sure as hell demanded that people slow down and gape. And somehow, I ended up behind this mountainous logging truck, which, by the way, I was very proud to see because I grew up around loggers. There was traffic crammed in all around my zones and I had a compromised following distance.

The worst part about this situation was that this poor spacing was accompanied by an even more miserable sight distance. I had no visual lead, and I couldn't see what was happening around in front of the logging truck. I couldn't pass him and there were idiots bearing down behind me as if the whole scenario was some preconceived concoction I had put together the night before, and punishing me for the inhumanity of it all. Bunch of primitive protruding brows and elongated jaws out there. And I know that the gentleman driving the truck could not see me, which I'm sure made him a little nervous. Although, I could have been dressed like Tarzan that day too, which could very well have made him nervous, I don't know. Maybe it was a blessing he couldn't see me. You think I'm joking. The day I did dress like Tarzan it was to promote our annual fundraiser jog-a-thon, and I got a first class sopping because we suddenly got a rain deluge of biblical proportions.

But there was very little I could to take myself out of this higher risk driving situation. I could not see where I was going, and I couldn't make any decisions about driving adjustments because all the clues in the traffic scene I am used to doing this with were simply out of my sight. *This* is what it is like for me teaching in a public school. Somehow, I can't make decisions about how to get myself out of these often futile conditions because I'm stuck simply bearing, or enduring the situation at hand. Some teachers know how to manage conditions better. I never learned, or I lacked the gene or something. It's frustrating for me to not see my effectiveness, to see what kind of change I am generating. It's not uncommon for me to want to *pull over*.

I drive like I live, usually very cautiously. And I know to live like this is not always a smart way to an enriched life. But I get scared. I like to keep my distance and see the entire traffic scene. I don't want to hastily make decisions because I know people can get hurt from that behavior, and I usually don't, but I certainly have in the past. I believe it is important to look ahead, and be ready for people who are coming on, and those who are leaving. And I have a heightened awareness of aggressive drivers. I do my best to abide by the spirit of cooperation.

Dan Powell

Driving is choosing safe travel paths and effective sightlines, all in the interest of facilitating good decision making. And it is not uncommon for me to examine and choose potential travel paths for my life while I drive. However, I rarely feel like I have clear sightlines. I spend the first third of my drive home shaking off the blows of the day's battle, and I am often too bleary eyed to see well enough into the future. This makes it very difficult to steer my life. Many of my teacher friends think I have this gift of philosophy to make connections in this way. My wife simply says I have a bad attitude, or that I'm arrogant. Then when I choose not to share because of this I'm passive aggressive. I desperately need to work on my communication skills, I guess. Besides, she's right more than I am by at least a 2 to 1 margin.

Many schools have as their mascot a hawk, symbolizing the predator-like qualities that they are so desirous to emulate as competitors on the ball fields and courts across America. It's the precision and the ferocity with which it unleashes itself upon animals of a lower rank in the natural selection sense of things. All of these, I have no doubt are true and hawks accurately reflect these qualities many wish to portray. But I see something else in these beautiful birds of prey, which by the way, are qualities that could also well represent sports teams. And it is more recognizable in one particular hawk.

Many times a week in the range of one drive, times a factor of .4 and .6, very near the state line if you remember correctly, I encounter a red-tailed hawk. He is perched on a freeway sign, or a fence post or a light pole, and he watches me drive by. And this occurs on the way home from, as well as to the school. He knows I'm there and he makes it a point to express his wisdom for me as he sees fit. Hawks have this uncanny sense of movement that is amazingly efficient. An economy of motion that proves I am an idiot for walking back and forth to and from the refrigerator sixteen times just to pour myself a glass of milk. Yet I have become more efficient in the classroom with my tool belt. Hawks never seem to waste movement. They always seem to be in control and exude this confidence, and this ability to communicate a trust in me. Every time I pass this guy, I notice that it is not a coincidence. I say outloud, "There's my hawk!" I need him for something and he answers me. He simply shows that he is there and that he knows the way, wherever I am "going".

I read an article in a magazine one time about this man and his classic car. He said that whenever he and his wife argued, that he would go out to the garage and sit in his car because it "understands" him. At the time I thought the guy was immature and not interested in growing up. I thought what kind of shallow mutton head sits in a car because it understands him? But it really isn't any different than what I find in nature and maybe I'm just now realizing that. A car seems to be materialistic while I have no desire to own a falcon or hawk. This man perhaps needs something to caress on the weekends with a soft towel. I need to know simply that nature is there, and if I look I can find answers to the big questions, and this is what this bird does for me. Although I know the answers are there, I do not always see them. They are like completely different portals to the same source. However, I believe mine is far superior than this guy's car. No offense to the man of course. Or perhaps I'm more immature than he; I really can't decide now.

Of course, there are thousands of hawks around and it is absurd to think that this particular hawk is the same one from previous encounters. I know this. But I can believe it is, and nobody will contradict that with counterexamples on my way to work. I am obliged only by my own imagination.

Some teachers who take themselves a little too seriously would think this is something that I need to share with my students. I say they would *think* I need to share, that is, if I told them about it. I would never tell other teachers about it. They would start jumping around with excitement throwing buzz words on top of my personal thoughts, and devising other ways they could absolutely destroy a perfect personal sensation of mine by attempting to teach it in a public school.

Please, I don't want to hear it if you think I'm too private. This is something that I would never share with my students. I already throw plenty of my pearls to them, and I don't need to assassinate my private peace on top of it all. I could never understand some teachers. They feel like you have to share everything in the class, and that no part of you shall be sandbagged, that all teachers are public domain. This is probably why I have an alter ego at school. I have constructed this character as a veneer. There are simply some things I want to keep. Movement on my travel path is mine.

My imagination is a great friend. My ideas can stir like the currents in a river and produce harm to no one. I realize that one of the great purposes of imagination is to reach out to others, and to improve humanity, to share the movement. Fishermen stand in a river baiting the fish. But teaching for me in the end, is deficient. I give a tremendous amount of creativity at my post, and I am lauded by some as gifted. But they don't know. What kind of gifted man can't manage his own sanity? Who am I to be extolled for walking the thin line between health and the desertion of my senses from time to time? I know it comes from expending too much of myself and I haven't yet learned to control it. Commuting and watching for the hawk allows me to recapture some of the pieces of myself that I give away. After all the bills are paid at school, I'm still slightly in the hole, but I can always find a few bits of loose change on my way home.

A Decline in Courage

He sat there in his chair and I wasn't sure that his feet were even touching the floor. He didn't smile much but he was always listening. He was left handed. He was short and slight of build, and he had a small gap between his teeth. There was nothing that Richard had that made him any more special than the average seventh grader. Most sports coaches weren't going to recruit him. He didn't seem to have an attractive personality, quiet kids usually don't. In fact if you didn't look closely, you could easily miss him. You might not even know that he was there. But there was an additional characteristic about Richard that one could easily look over, and that is the fact that *he knew he was there.* This is what he came to our school with, and this is what sustained him through middle school. This is really all that mattered to him at the time, and this is why he left as King Richard.

In a way, Richard reminded me of a small dog that my wife and I had one time that we originally inherited from a psychopathic megalomaniacal girlfriend-beating law school student. We are convinced he is out in the world today winning awards from associations that are just as destructive as he is. Maybe even the ACLU. I will let this particular strand of the story rest right there. Nonetheless, the brain of all of our ten pound dog was convinced that she was just as capable, just as fast, and just as high in the food chain as any other mammal on the planet. She was confident that she could express herself to her complete capacity. If dogs can do this, why can't all people? This is how Richard led his life.

All through the school year he was very diligent in his work. He made an effort to be neat, he made an effort to be thorough, and he made an effort to learn. I wouldn't describe him as an outstanding student, although he seemed to be very strong in math. It was always his essence that marked him as a different kid. When it came time for track and field in the spring, Richard turned out. My good friend Ron Knudsen and I were coaching, and this pleased us tremendously because we needed any bodies out for the team. I knew Richard would be a hard worker. And track and field at the middle school level was a sport where a kid would never have to ride the pine. There was no such thing as starting players or substitutes, everyone just went out and did their events.

As it turned out, King Richard didn't surprise us because he went out everyday and did his workouts with an intensity that matched everything else he put his mind to. There was very little hope that Richard was going to score any points that season. He had no speed, no strength and no jumping ability. Nothing. But he didn't need it because he had something else. He had himself.

We noticed something very unusual that year while working with him. He ran with his eyebrows crunched inward, like his very life depended on it. He would turn a corner and run by some of the other kids who were yanking each other's sweats down and generally acting their age or younger, probably younger. These kids would stop and stare at him running by, not making a peep, with their sweats still down around their ankles. They noticed something about King Richard. They didn't know what it was and they didn't discuss it because they simply weren't equipped. They just watched him run around the track for another quarter lap like he was their king, yet, not knowing how to articulate this. He was indeed a king.

You see, Richard could care less if he was called the lone lame duck on the planet. And he could care less if he drew your attention. His prime mover was to do something that he never had done in his life, perhaps run a little faster or jump a little farther than *he* was able to do before. This was probably best demonstrated at the track and field championship meet, in which he barely qualified for the long jump in his class. Actually it was in the qualifying meet that preceded the championship meet. Of course Richard didn't qualify that day, but it didn't matter. His own inner guide was not concerned with this.

I'm almost positive that Richard had the shortest long jump in the entire district that season. Mr. Justh, the science teacher from my school, had graciously volunteered to run the long jump pit. He was that type of marvelous teacher that gently teased his students with a twinkle in his eye. I overheard him telling Richard, "What are you doing over here Richard? You're not going to win this, look at all these bigger kids out here." Richard looked up at him with his signature intensity and his eyebrows crunched in and gently replied, "What does that have to do with anything?"

This drew a gentle chuckle from Mr. Justh because he was just as aware of Richard's gift as the rest of us. And

Richard also knew he was doing it out of support. I stood next to Richard when this incident occurred and I specifically remember that witnessing his reaction was special. I felt like someone had cracked a door for me to get a peek at something that was normally kept under wraps, something that if it got out would make everyone want to have it. When everyone has something, it's not as valuable anymore. But for some reason, I was afforded a short, furtive glance.

It was only at this time that I realized that I never met either of Richard's parents. They never showed up at the meets. I needed to know whose influence it was that was behind this kid. So, I did some sleuthing and discovered that earlier in the year he woke up and his mom was gone. She had decided that she didn't want to be married anymore nor be a mom, so she left. The father remained but had to get a second job to support the kids, which is why he could never make it to the track meets. Richard left immediately after practice to go home and make his younger siblings dinner and help get them ready for bed. He also got them ready in the mornings. Richard had himself, and he supported himself in every way he could think of, and he improved his life every day that he got up and tried. Long live the king. It is kids like these that really get me thinking. What makes him choose to be the way he is when others choose differently? Why do kids not always choose the high road?

And then one day I stepped out of my classroom to help monitor the passing time between classes and as I did so, something passed my face that sounded like a hummingbird. A few minutes later Mike Fosburg, a fellow math teacher and great friend and confidant, told me he caught a kid throwing nails down the hall and confronted him about being dangerous. Apparently one whizzed by his face and, I don't know, I think he was being a little hard on the kid don't you think? He was just a youngster and writing him up and referring him to the office really wasn't going to help his esteem any. And so it goes in public school. I thought for a minute that Mike was wasting his time and then dismissed that thought because throwing nails is probably considered some type of assault or even using a weapon. But a few days later Mike told me that his "case" was indeed dismissed by the PC Administravia Protectorship as one in which no punishment could be handed down. The kid had an I.E.P. which means that he can run the school in any fashion he chooses. An Individual Education Plan and being in the resource room are synonymous. No form of consequence, apparently, could be lowered on this kid because doing so would be unfair to his "disorder". And then I think of the "disorder" in the life of young King Richard, and others just like him showing up everyday with disadvantages. It makes me sick to my stomach to know who is really getting the shaft here.

I don't know if this was flimsy state or district policy or just the flimsy spine of the Protectorship, and at the time it didn't matter to me. Actually, it still doesn't matter to me. It's all part of the tentacles of the system that have grown to choke everything else around it. It all comes out of this deed we think we are doing for kids who are otherwise intolerable, and attempting to make them believe that if we show that we care, he will miraculously turn his life around.

But in the meantime, the decent kids walking down the hall that day became just a little more bitter at a system that's supposed to be the best education experience in the world. All I was capable of feeling at the time was that everything was really upside down. We had become so tolerant of all conditions and all people that personal safety was something that only a bigot would value.

Not acknowledging the "disorders" of these hallway primates resulted in labeling yourself an impudent, insensitive ignoramus. It is a time where we tolerate the bullies. We tolerate the dangers. We tolerate the violence and reward the stupidity. And we do this while not even patting the backs of the kids like Richard.

I remember this day, because when Mike informed me of the result of his effort to make the hallways safe, I stopped monitoring the hallway between classes. I figured I wasn't going to waste my time. Never had anything seemed so backward and so worthlessly stupid in the public schools, at least this particular school at the time. And I know we weren't the worst school. It is ugly and frustrating to try so hard to achieve a positive change, and know that nothing will happen.

One time the PC Administravia Protectorship told all the teachers at a staff meeting that there were two or three kids who were out of control in the hall before and between classes. The Protectorship wanted all teachers to stand out in the hall and monitor, and if anybody looked suspicious, to nail them. We asked this entity why not just tell us *who* the kids were, and we could watch *them* instead. The Protectorship replied, "Well, I can't do that." I guess this governing body figured that would be profiling. Makes me want to scream. I've seen public swimming pools run better.

A couple of years before this, I had a girl tell me, "Kiss my ass!" with plenty of volume and spirit. I wrote it up for this same official, you know, referred her to the office. The official's first act was to immediately come down to my room and start interviewing kids sitting around her to see if that's what she really said. I guess my word was not good without the corroboration of a quorum of thirteen year-olds. You can see, of course, how this strengthened my credibility with the kids, you know. They could see just how much the administration trusted my perspective.

I have never been in a casino. I don't think I have anyway. I have read about how they have been designed entirely with the customer in mind, the gambler. Albeit, I don't think gambling attracts the smallest numbers of seedy people. It doesn't matter for this example. Oxygen is pumped into the rooms, the furniture and the tables are ergonomically designed. They are waited and doted upon, and wooed. They are given a chance to maintain and inspire hope. Their senses are massaged (as well as their wallets), and they are made to feel welcome. The gambling business knows their customers well and they attend to them in an astonishingly expert fashion. Why are schools not designed like this? I mean, at least the oxygen thing. That would be a damn good idea. We constantly look the other way, ignoring the idiots who need serious behavior management intervention as well as dismissing the heroic efforts of our kings. It is my opinion everybody loses in public schools because of this. It's demoralizing to kids. It's demoralizing to teachers.

Every garden has the issue of weeds to contend with, but they are carefully managed to allow the proper growth of purposeful and virtuous plants. Schools let anything grow. Schools aren't interested in developing the type of environment where only high virtue is the goal, because doing so would be casting a prejudicial frown on the *diversity* of others and what we call a virtue here is not necessarily are virtue there. No one has the firmness to say what it is we value, because we value *everything!* When everything is valued, nothing is valued!

I was at a party one time, there were many people standing around amidst loud chatter and this one girl walked in and exclaimed, "Hi, everybody!" Maybe one person who was near the door might have acknowledged her and I thought to myself, she didn't say hi to anybody. When you say hi to everybody, you say hi to nobody. And it is my opinion that in the public schools, it is a contest to see how many people we can say hi to. Yes, I know that we are in the people business, that we need to serve and develop people. But is anybody aware that there is a point of diminishing returns? That we bend toward and tolerate so many "disorders" that never "existed" until recently? That there are kids out there like King Richard that struggle and succeed anyway? That we are actually making it more difficult for more kids? It doesn't matter to me that Richard didn't have a "diagnosis". He could've gone out and ordered one like everyone else. But what made him immensely different is that *he didn't.* He wasn't looking for one. All he wanted was a chance to try. Like I said, it makes me sick to my stomach to know that we put our boot heels on his neck by letting the primates chuck nails down the hall.

There are so many adults out there who are searching desperately for a medical excuse for their children. "There must be *something* that's wrong with him that is not our fault!" I wish these parents could hear how many times a year that teachers hear, "Oh, he has A.D.D." (Or A.D.H.D., or O.D.D. or B.F.D. or a thousand different excuses.) To me, this is what they are, excuses. People are always looking for a way to lower the expectations, to find the justification not to meet the same academic or behavior standards that everyone else is responsible for meeting. It makes me crazy! Yeah, of course I know some of you are saying, "Well, Powell's no doctor. He earned himself a D in college biology." I don't care; it was a group of medical doctors that enlightened me of the sham in the first place. Some parents think that because their kid is disruptive in class, it means he's a genius. Kids are just being kids. They need exciting learning choices and opportunities but they need managed! Especially in social contexts!

There is often a thick dark line between courage and stupidity, and another one between having a good attitude and being very honest. Public schools have found neither. I'm not sure they want to find them with all the smearing of the lines with cowardice and accommodation. Where has our courage gone that used to let us support the right choices?

My mother used to tell us that when she was in school, her social worth went from low class ridicule to pass over. She was teased and abused by other kids until, in the end, she was ignored, perhaps a worse fate. A least gaining some attention might have some worth. So it is with many students in our system, we ignore or undervalue all core values because we are clogged up in federal mandates and accommodations. As long as the kids come to work the best they can, *regardless of any difficulties,* they will be ignored by our system because we throw all of our attention toward rewarding stupidity, acknowledging excuses and supporting low achievement. That's all. Nowadays, anybody can order up a disorder (thanks to Section 504 of a Federal "Civil Rights" statute enacted in the early 1970s) and have the entire school system hopping around waiting on him hand and foot.

We had a kid in one of our schools who had his own personal secretary funded by the tax payers of course. Her job was to follow him around and keep him organized. The "rationale" behind this was that the poor kid had some lame attention "disorder". She followed him from class to class reminding him to behave like all the others and picked up anything he dropped and prompted him to organize it. Forget about getting the parents and the kid to acknowledge an obstacle, *which we all have,* and giving him strategies for *overcoming it.* That is out of the question. We exacerbate the problem by excusing it, drawing attention to it, and showing all the other kids in the school what they too could have if they could just get their parents to sign up for a disorder at the office of their family physician.

Another kid actually had the audacity to threaten to kill another teacher at my school. This teacher told me directly that he looked at her and said, "I'm going to kill you." Well, as it turned out nobody could even look at the kid funny for doing it because he had an I.E.P. for one class. Absolutely amazing. Nothing could be done because he was a resource room student. I told the teacher that if she decided not to return to school until he was gone I would not return either. I was fully prepared to express myself. Although in retrospect this would've made my wife furious with me. She's okay with people taking a stand as long as it's not me, for family reasons no doubt. My rebuttal might be that I need to take a stand for family reasons too. Remaining a living father tends to help keep the family together.

I was sitting in a "student study" session listening to another case about a student I personally had absolutely no trouble with whatsoever. She was perhaps a little slower to understand and a little quirky, but she was a kid! Doesn't that naturally characterize certain people? Especially if they are not yet done developing? When they're still doughy in the middle? No, say the intervention specialists. They, along with some gullible parents and scheister doctors will find some "disorder" to slap on them no matter how normal conditions seem. They are determined to find some cruel disadvantage that fate has bestowed upon them. They conjure up disorders with such frequency it's difficulty to keep track of them. This one they told me was O.D.D. Oppositional Defiance Disorder. I broke down, chuckling like I was choking on the ingenious invention of this one. I *sincerely* thought they were joking! Only when they stared at me, offending their professionalism, did I realize that they were dead serious. Their tone is this: This is her disorder dammit and here's what you better be doing to accommodate her in the classroom you s.o.b. unless you want to go against the law. And if you do that you ignorant bigot, you are going to be hearing from the attorneys.

This particular accommodation plan called for us teachers to talk gently to her, and always give her as many options as necessary so as not to aggravate her, and above all, do not raise the level of your voice because this could send her spiraling toward low achievement. You have no idea how sick these people made me. They know the kid's rights but no one else's. And I know what they're thinking.

"Mr. Powell, there is actually a difference between *accommodation* and *modification!*" Yeah, yeah I know. We get beaten with this at least once a year in staff meetings: accommodation doesn't (shouldn't) affect learning outcome, and modification does. So what? (And while I'm at it, all of this is my *opinion.* I have to say this so that all the mad dog educators out there can back down and take a breather, and give the foam around there mouths a chance to dry up and drop off.)

Other kids' plans require assignments cut in half from the other kids, because they lose focus, or letting them sit wherever they damn well please. Keep this one away from too much stimuli, keep that one away from the quiet because they have a quiet disorder. Let this one come to class whenever they feel like it because they have an I-get-lost-at school-disorder. Don't yell at this one because he's a bully and you might make him upset. Let this one leave the room anytime because he's not potty trained. *I don't care if he is smoking cigarettes in the bathroom, you bigot! You are just insensitive to kids. You just don't care about kids.* She has to sit up front; he has to sit by himself. You need to give him his assignments in writing everyday because he can't write. You have to read for this kid his because he can't read. And whatever you do, don't forget about her. She needs to be prompted no less than 37 times before you can move on to the next level of action. And Mr. Powell, that's 37 times for one issue such as kicking the student in front of her. When a separate issue arises, start counting over or separately. By the way, Mr. Powell, standardized test scores are down so let's get cracking.

In a nutshell, making excuses for and catering to the inept, without giving them strategies to overcome is forsaking the rest of our kids who are trying their hearts out. It is upside down, pathetic, stupid and dangerous. Didn't Abraham Lincoln say something about cutting off the body to save the arm is not a smart thing to do?

504 accommodation plans usually went from the meetings to my hands to the nearest wastebasket. I think they were invented by a bunch of bandits who think all teachers are a geminy of baboons who can be duped. I became so exhausted with these accommodations that I made up one of my own disorders. I figured everyone else was making them up. I call my 504 disorder not A.D.D. or O.D.D., but S.H.A.F.T.E.D. The Sick of the Hog-Assed Fat Talkers

of Educationese Disorder. It is characterized by students who experience frustrations at having teacher attention be deferred to students with other 504 accommodations. So to accommodate these kids we are going to let them have their own passing time between classes and allow them to not be within 100 feet of students with other 504 "disorders". In effect, they would be segregated from the "helpless" idiots *that the rest of us make worse by excusing their shortcomings, instead of teaching them to adapt, modify, overcome and improvise!* Isn't that the whole point of education?

But we don't. We much prefer to keep the problem as far removed from the solution as possible. Somehow they will magically know how to do these things as an adult. Just look the other way, close your eyes and wish really, really hard.

What is happening? What if this were sports, the life focus of western civilization? Haven't we all seen or read about deaf track participants, one-armed wrestlers and one-legged football players? Nobody gives them head starts. Nobody gives them a "w" before the contest begins to salvage their "esteem". Haven't I heard their parents say how proud they are of their efforts? Don't they actually *want* to be treated like the others?

If I was a kid today, this is what I would do to take over the school and run it my way. I would whine to my parents that I'm not being challenged in school. That the boring lessons make me fidgety and I find my attention being drawn to other things. Bingo. My mom would have me in to some shallow, arrogant physician who would then drug me up higher than a kite for some sham disorder. By the way, check to see how many school children are drugged up everyday by prescriptions in this country before they come to school and compare it to other nations. You may be surprised. And yes, as a matter of fact, I do believe that ninety percent of these things are made up.

Anyway, next I would complain about how unfairly I'm treated at the school and that I'm being singled out. That because I got caught calling a girl a whore, all the other boys that called girls whores that day were not caught, and therefore, I'm being picked on and singled out and this school is fascist and unconstitutional. After this little episode, I would start spreading rumors about how my dad is the white man's Jessie Jackson and he's going to see to it that he shakes down all the idiot teachers and administrators, because the school staff is a bunch of pre-judicial hate mongers. This of course will bring the public school system to a feverish hand-wringing session because the last thing a liberal run organization would want to be called is hateful by its own pawns.

Presto. The school officials would be running scared and would have long been looking the other way if I wanted to call a girl a whore again, and consequently, I run the school. The best part about it is that the kids know who runs the school too.

Where on earth has common sense gone?

Then we have the issue of self-esteem to deal with. Teachers are funny about this. You should see teachers' reactions when they hear someone's self-esteem is endangered. A child's self-esteem that is. They could care less about my esteem or morale. They drop everything they're doing and run around like epileptic hens. "Save him, save him! Ahhhhhhhh!" Every time a teacher tells me that a kid needs a higher self-esteem I always say, "You mean like Adolph Hitler? His was very high. So was that of Eric Harris and Dylan Kliebold at Columbine High School.

They had great self-esteem." (Incidentally, weren't those two monsters supposed to be "gifted"?)

Here I am being ignorant, arrogant, and insensitive again. I should just forget about it. What am I going to do about it anyway? The agony is sometimes too much to handle. I don't have it in me to stand by and watch the other kids try, that's all. It is heartbreaking. With all the idiots we surround them with, and the burdens we force on them I'm surprised they last as long as they do. I guess we feel they have enough as it is. Don't think these kids are unaware of it either. On more than one occasion I've had students come up to me after school and say, "Why do all the bad kids get all the teachers' attention?" I shake my head at them and answer the best way I know how, "You wouldn't believe me if I told you." I am a nobody. I am only one man.

The welfare approach to education is not the answer I know that. The "less" a kid has the more they don't have to do. That's it. If I could wave my magic wand, here's how I would fix it: First, I would immediately get rid of the sugar machines. After that, I would wipe out the militant teacher unions that do nothing but tell me and all the other teachers how to think politically. "Here, you're not smart enough because you're a teacher. So, here's what we want you to think about the war in Iraq…" They are always in our faces about many things that have nothing to do with education. Then I would double the pay of those teachers I thought were making a substantial difference on standardized test scores, test scores against national if not international norms that is. And subsequently launch a massive recruiting campaign to develop a talented pool of teachers who could teach kids *how to think critically,* and how to adhere to a language of accountability. But to do it in a dynamic way that suits their talents. After that, I would abolish the acknowledgement of the useless 504 accommodations (ninety percent of them) and redefine what special education means so they don't include frivolous or made up "disabilities". The focus of teaching would be thinking critically and creatively, learning the language of accountability, and the means of adapting, overcoming, modifying, and improvising. Critical thinking is absolutely gone from public school. It has been at least partially beaten out by the allure of moronic, sense-dulling video games and exceedingly stupid television programming.

That's it. That's all I'm saying. I'm already going to be bullied by the ACLU for comments I made earlier, and now the NEA (National Education Association) is going to send over Moose and Rocko to my door some night. If you see me with broken fingers or if I suddenly disappear with no trace, investigate these two organizations first. Actually, it could be a parent group from a small town in Eastern Washington but check the other two first.

I find it in my nature to help a kid, most teachers do. That's why we became teachers in the first place! But the kid doesn't know any better. And most teachers are willing to help him without the kid having some label slapped on him by scheisters. I prefer them all to be labeled "kid", and let us go from there. Sometimes, I see this as the problem: I see kids while the others see pupils. It would most certainly be helpful if the kid tries to be coachable in the first place. (How do you teach a kid to be *coachable?*)

I sometimes wonder whatever happened to King Richard. He's out there somewhere, hopefully motivating others to put out their best efforts. That is a true contribution to society, to inspire others to put out their best. As a teacher, it's an essential trait to encourage this but it does not always happen. There are a great many factors involved in achievement besides good motivation and inspiration. Still, to be able to do so would be a wonderful contribution. By my own admission, I don't know how to do it. Right now I think I am partially effective in some cases and most of the time this is what I can reasonably expect. Many teachers have an inflated sense of their effectiveness, which is not good either. Richard had something. Maybe it's *that* I should be pursuing instead.

We ask the impossible of our students, especially middle school kids. We ask them to sit still and be quiet all day and then we torture them with boring tasks. No wonder they go bananas during passing times. But here's where I may be different. Depending on the task, I think there is value to be derived out of this. Math is a great example. Because a kid thinks a topic is boring and arduous doesn't guarantee that it has no value. We can attempt to flavor these things but nothing is going to prevent all kids from declaring its uselessness. I believe a limited amount of force feeding is in order. Kids don't know what is best, that's why they should and do look to knowledgeable and experienced people for leadership. Unfortunately, not all parents or teachers are that way.

Giving kids excuses masked as 504 accommodations as well as a host of others is going to do as much damage to a kid's natural ability and desire to learn and succeed as drugs do. Yet, putting them *on* drugs is how we combat this! I cannot understand this! Will somebody please help me? (I could re-write *Alice in Wonderland* and set it in a public school.) Overcoming failure is an essential process that builds a desire to not only achieve, but to see the world as it really is. And that is as a place that will eventually confront us with conditions of challenge and difficulty. But, there are others out there more powerful than me spreading the message that nothing we see is reality, that everything is an interpretation.

Accommodations for children in the order of allowing them to do less, or to be less, or even to behave less are putting small stones on a pile. Every time they hear it from us that they "don't have to do it", or that they are "disabled" puts another stone on this pile of belief that they are not capable of accomplishing things as others are. Someday the pile gets so enormous that it can't be moved. Their lack of belief can't be shaken and it becomes even harder to achieve positive change. You watch. We'll be driving achievement even lower until the sense of entitlement changes. We should be ashamed. It reminds me of *Brave New World* and personally, I think it's criminal.

At the Edge of the Cliff

Life's tests. Sometimes we beg for them without even being fully aware of it. The depressing thing about big mistakes is when you recognize them as wrong before you even embark on the misadventure itself. Sometimes a fella is out to get himself, in spite of himself and ends up dragging everyone down to the gutter with him. I wish I was talking about someone else, especially after expressing my thoughts on kids who drag the system down.

I am always telling my math students how Shakespeare's characters are full of madness like Hamlet and King Lear. And then there's Macbeth, who seemed almost as normal as the rest of us until he got swept away with his deal. Actually, Othello wasn't exactly a straight thinker either. All of these characters met with an unpleasant end. And a few years ago, I let myself get carried off by my own misjudgment and insanity. Luckily though, I didn't end up in a pile of bodies. Nor was I certifiably insane, but I did follow the stupid path all the way to the edge of the cliff. So why was I fond of telling my students about these unfortunate characters as if they were models to avoid, when it turned out I was a parallel character with parallel stupidity? I don't know. I'm trying to figure it out still.

I had a friend in the latter part of my college "career" who was preparing himself to be a trader at the Chicago Mercantile Exchange. I didn't even know what he was talking about half the time when he described it. You're probably getting red flags right now. Your senses are tingling, I can tell. Anytime someone says he doesn't know what someone is talking about half the time, you can bet that it's more like most of the time.

Steve Olson was a guy I admired because he seemed to be naturally intelligent and he worked hard as well. Although he was my age, I suppose he was a role model for my own pursuits. Usually I think of role models as having to be older than me. You know, someone with years of experience behind their words of advice and counsel. Not that he was a bad guy though. He was quite the opposite. We trained in the gym together and he had an eclectic and sharp sense of humor.

He moved to Chicago and realized his dream of working as a trader and as far as I could tell, met with relative success as evidenced by his nice apartment and a boat he owned with a friend for outings on Lake Michigan. We talked from time to time and he spoke of up days and down days, and for the most part I did not fully comprehend what he was doing.

A few years later he died just shy of his thirtieth birthday. Obviously this very much took me by surprise. According to his parents with whom I corresponded, he lied down for a nap and didn't wake up. Nothing showed up on the autopsy report and the incident went down as a mystery as far as I know. Of course it was tragic. The man hadn't even really begun, and again, I admired how sharp and gentlemanly he was. I relayed this to his parents when I wrote them after his death.

It was a couple of years after this that I found a book. It was a self teaching method for trading commodities in the futures markets, the area in which Steve worked. And since it supposedly shed light on what was a mysterious activity to me, it caught my interest. It should've been subtitled *How To Run Up $45,000 of Credit Card Debt and Make Your Wife Take The Kids And Run.* To be honest, the book certainly didn't recommend borrowing money to do this. That was a product of my own genius. More on that in a moment.

Anyway, why I noticed it in the first place was that this is what Steve was into and he seemed like a sharp guy. The problem was, he wasn't around to consult, and I'm sure his involvement in the business didn't risk his own borrowed capital. He was employed by someone else but to this day I do not know the connection between what he did and how he was paid.

I studied the book thoroughly and learned more about the potential in trading commodities and decided that it would be a great way to pay off my $22,000 student loan debt. I decided that I would borrow money against my credit cards, jump in to the market and leap out by the end of the month and return the money before the finance charges were posted. Additionally, I "perfected" this wonderful idea by not telling my wife. I fantasized that one day soon I could tell her my student loan debts were gone, and I could do so over a nice dinner and a glass of wine. And as this brilliant plan of mine unfolded, it had wrinkle after wrinkle in it that most people except me would've seen long before it was ever taken off the shelf.

As with many naïve novices, I met with pleasing initial success. I had "made" about $10,000 in the first six weeks jumping in and out of cattle and corn futures, and felt confident I was going to be having that dinner with my wife sooner than I anticipated. Incidentally, I discovered that "making" money in this fashion creates an absolutely empty feeling. Since I didn't trade any service or product for it, I felt as if I didn't deserve it because it was not earned. It was a very empty, empty feeling, although I was not quick to realize this. Someone who does this and this only to make money is sure to soon meet with a counselor and a bottle of Prozac. Maybe this is something that no one else on the planet would believe unless he experienced himself, but it's the absolute truth. It does nothing for authentic self-esteem or achievement.

Trading commodities is not like investing in the stock market. In the stock market, you can only lose what you initially invest. If it drops to zero, that's it, it's over, and you lose your money and move on. With commodities, you can lose more than the money you put up front in the first place and end up owing more money through "margin calls", which is the amount that keeps you vested in your position without making the traders and brokers nervous.

Well, as any outsider looking in could've predicted, I eventually met with disaster. I was always on an ice flow moving in the wrong direction. It was like my dog that was always on the wrong side of the door. Simply put, it was a dumb decision in the first place, and when the dumb decision manifested itself into this predicament, I panicked and astoundingly became dumber.

I kept getting these margin calls to stay in the position until the market swung the other way, and I just kept borrowing and borrowing on my credit cards hoping that the nightmare would end around the corner. I jumped from corn to cattle, to soy beans to lumber, back to corn again, abandoning every strategy I read about. There was margin call after margin call. I went in deeper and deeper, and I began panicking, not believing this was happening to me. It all had to stop when all the cards were maxed out. I would pay our bills and there would be very little left over after making payments to six or seven banks for the credit. And then the top knot on this mess-I cashed out part of my wife's IRA thinking I could pay it all back to help eliminate this debt, which was even more nonsensical because it didn't even cover a fraction of what I owed. I also cashed out part of our kids' small college savings, part of which was started by Julie's parents thinking I could pay it back too. All of this, remember, was done unbeknownst to Julie. I paid on the debts for a couple months until I literally got sick. We had almost no money left over at the end of the month to live on.

That was it. I couldn't take it any longer. I couldn't stand that squalid feeling of knowing what I was doing was wrong. I remember it was a Tuesday on April 6 that I told Julie everything, and naturally, she was devastated with me...again. How many times in a man's life can he disappoint his wife? When all the accounts came in, I owed more than $45,000 in credit card debt, and any trust Julie had in me at the time was gone. In fact, there was a "margin call" there too. I didn't tell Julie for three weeks after that I had actually cashed out part of her IRA, and that pulled me deeper in to emotional debt than I ever imagined the financial debt would be. It was quite honestly one of the worst acts of selfishness and deceit one can do in a relationship. I was embarrassed, dejected and had no self-confidence left in me, and the dinner with wine was certainly not going to happen. I had purposefully whipped around the corner in a reckless skid and came to a stop on Deep Shit Drive.

All this time, I was teaching school and I had to show up everyday and be a model

of confidence and a pillar of strength for my students. You know, all the students I was working so hard to get good decisions out of? I was a fraud. This was as enormous of a problem as everything else that I buried myself under. Julie could hardly stand to look at me, or even our own children without feeling like she betrayed them because of being with me. I told my principal at the time that I wasn't sure, but I thought that I would be losing my family soon and divorce may be around the corner. And also, that I wasn't sure how long I could be a teacher because of what I did. I didn't feel I could pretend to be a model for them when I couldn't even be one for my own family. To my principal's credit, she was very encouraging and tried to present me with the qualities I had remaining that were positive for teaching. They went in one ear and out the other. There I was, at the edge of the cliff and hanging on for dear life.

I have absolutely no idea how we made it through the first six months of this ordeal. That first summer I know that two or three times we were one sentence away from getting divorced. Everything was there except the words: the looks, the overtones, and the condescension. The timing was also horrible because we were selling our single wide trailer and moving into, well, I didn't know at the time. We already had a buyer for it and we had no place to go. And who was going to lend money to a man who had a car loan, a computer loan, student loans (now whittled down to $12,000 from $22,000…whoopee.) no savings, no confidence and $45,000 of unsecured debt on top of it all?

This is the greatest country on the planet. A mortgage company did come through with a plan they approved, although it meant a higher interest rate than the current market rate, and a balloon payment at the end of fifteen years. I also had to borrow some money from my brother and his wife for the down payment. This too was humiliating. Everybody in our family and our circle of friends eventually found out what I did. I did care about the debt, but I could've cared less if the entire world knew at that point. I was going to have myself busy repaying the debt, not worrying about what the world thought about me. I already knew what they thought and I couldn't change it anyway.

We were lucky because it looked as if all we could afford were the shacks in the methamphetamine neighborhoods, but we discovered a nice little newer house in a decent neighborhood. It was 930 square feet of charm and quite cheery looking. Looking back on this, maybe we should've rented a place for less and doubled up on some payments. My wife was already prepared to do the burning bed trick on me again and she was damned if she was going to lower her own standard of living because of my doing. So what was I going to say? Financial advice coming from me was going to go over like unsupervised sixth graders with a can of spray paint. On top of all this our daughter picked up lice somewhere. And my wife picked up a louse along the way too, if you know what I mean.

I visited a counselor for the next year at my wife's request and I heard myself tell her that I felt like I was at the bottom of a canyon with rocks piled on top of me with no one to turn to that would help. (Did I describe my Air Force Academy experience this way?) There was only me and it was the loneliest time of my life. I was the only one who could untie this knot. What I did was an unforgivable, cowardly, and rotten thing to do to my own wife and kids.

It was a very long first year. We enrolled in this counseling service for credit card debt and naturally cut up all the cards. It was degrading. They talked to us like we were ignorant and uneducated, although they did attempt to provide some dignity. And I had to put Julie through this treatment because, again, of my marvelous decision-making skills. I took a job as a carpenter's helper over the summer which was good because I left early in the morning and came home only when I had to because I know Julie needed to be away from me. School was out for the summer, and I also had to line up some type of weekend job for the school year before it arrived. I spent the entire first summer working in the heat and the dust convinced that I was going to be a single dad who only got to see his kids every other weekend. I hate the heat and the dust even without those other thoughts.

I found it ironic that part of my job that summer was to "clean out" these two old cabins, get rid of all the "garbage" that was inside of them, decontaminate the "rodent nests", tear out the ceilings, "sweep" all the "debris" away, dump it all into a truck and drive it to the "landfill" where it was to be destroyed by burial. I then had to "sweep" again, "vacuum, bleach, and disinfect" everything all the way down to the studs in their "walls", the very basic forms that "held this structure together so it was useful to other people". I was starting over...again.

Also that summer, I picked up some temporary work for a few days here and a few days there through an agency. I always showed up with some other skuzzy looking people, and the managers would always come out to this group and announce loudly, "I need to know which one of you is the teacher!" You could tell all of those in the group who hated school and their teachers when they were younger, they were always the ones snickering as I raised my hand, and muttering things about me not being so smart after all. One of my first temp jobs was spending three days in the basement of this dreary and smelly plastics-mold factory. I had to grind up all this useless plastic in this giant machine chopper. I actually thought a couple of times about doing Julie a favor and jumping in it myself. My supervisor was a former student of my wife's when she taught high school. He was a slacker in school and skipped out on many of his classes, including Julie's choir class. I'm not even sure he finished high school and I had a masters degree. This was the guy who was going to check my work. He knew exactly who I was, and didn't say a word to me the entire three days. After I discovered he was going to be my supervisor, I thought again about jumping into the chopper. Although I worked alone the vast majority of the time there, he occasionally drove by in a forklift and stared at me. That was delightful, absolutely delightful.

For the school year, I picked up this job pressure washing tractors and trailers with a small crew of two or three others beside myself. It turned out to be good work, with a good crew of guys. Although it was only a few dollars an hour, it felt right that it should be cheap because I felt cheap at the time. It was an all day job on Saturdays and I got picked up at 5 a.m. and was usually gone for twelve to fourteen hours. This was also good for Julie. I'm sure when her friends asked her how everything was going, she would reply that the "thing" was not only going, but he was gone. And that's the way it went for that particular school year.

As time went on, I developed an affinity for working at something that was entirely different than teaching. It was much more physical and I learned about another set of people that had a different set of values than most of the teachers I knew. These guys went out and enjoyed their work, not that teachers don't, and were very efficient at their trade. Efficiency was something that was just shy of totally alien to me in the education world, so it served also as a good reminder that the rest of the world isn't necessarily on the same track as teaching. Over the course of time, I learned to bring these characteristics into my classroom and I became more results oriented. This is not easy to do in teaching.

The best part of the day was usually all the work we did before noon. It was especially enjoyable that first late summer and early fall when the weather was so glorious. Getting a little water in your face was exhilarating, but the day grew very tiresome from noon on. I always showed up back at home absolutely filthy and physically spent. All the dirt and grime that was on the vehicles inevitably got rinsed back on to us, and it smelled horrible too.

As the autumn deepened the job began to turn gruesome. It had to. Up to this point I was working for extra money to put food on the table. Just to survive. My payments to my creditors were over $800 a month. This was more than our house payment. All this extra work so I could send $800 dollars a month to someone else. Someday when it would all be over, I would have nothing to show for it. This is what I should've been doing to eliminate my student loans in the first place. There had to be another point for me where it was so miserable that it would push me over the edge, a complete paradigm shift, just as the squalid feelings inside of me pushed me to tell Julie that night all the damage I did. There had to be more changes and another one was on the way, I remember, as we continued washing into the winter. I could feel it coming on.

I remember it was around the winter solstice. It had long been dark and we had headlamps mounted on our heads so we could see. We were doing a set of tractor-trailers out by an airport. It was snowing and the wind was blowing wet flakes sideways through my ears. The torn and wet wool gloves on my hands provided little protection and my fingers were so cold that they remained stiff and curled even after I let go of the thick- handled scrub brush I used to break the dirt loose from under the snow accumulating on the trucks. They began to swell. They looked arthritic, like I couldn't let go of a steering wheel. A steering wheel, I thought, how odd. In these conditions, a burner, or heater, was utilized on the pressure washer water. Yet, it was only effective at greater than or equal to 25 degrees. Things were starting to frost over which made it even more difficult to scrub. Nobody talked. We were all cold, tired and silent. I had school work that had been building up and all I ever felt like doing on my one day off was to sleep. And even though I was on my Christmas break I knew I was going to have to produce even more effort on that end of things just to keep from being too far behind, let alone caught up. And there was probably about another hour of work left. That would make it about 8:30 p.m. when we finished, I thought. We had been on the move since 5 a.m.

We weren't even done with this particular job yet, and I remember there really wasn't a good time for me to be reflective and contemplative. We worked fast. Yet, this feeling came over me from somewhere that night that I had it in me to redefine myself. I didn't have to be out there with nothing in front of me but paying off my debt and feeding my family. There's a lot more I could be doing. Right out there in the middle of this snow storm that night, in the dark except for some skinny beams of light bouncing around, I changed. I felt this warm light inside my chest and stomach, and I became a little giddy. Perhaps it was the brutality of the cold that was making me delirious. But I had an idea. I looked at my curled hands. I was going to somehow save enough money, above and beyond what I was making, over the winter and spring and invest in *myself* so I could go to summer school. I was not going to be washing trucks anymore. I was not going to grind plastic, and I was not going to flirt with bankruptcy or divorce any longer. I was going to win back the trust and confidence my wife had lost in me. In the middle of that snowy job, I decided that I was going to pay off my debt in three and a half more years, not five and a half. I smiled inside of my body for the next hour and I smiled the entire forty five minute drive back home. I think it was belief that was knocking at me from the inside. I wondered if this is what King Richard felt. And with my hands up in front of me, still stuck like I was hanging on to an invisible idea, I decided that I was going change everything by teaching high school students how to drive.

What a strange time to consider such drastic measures. Surely I was safer in what I was currently doing. Maybe it *was* the cold. My friend Mike Fosburg, the band teacher, had told me that he was swamped as a drivers education teacher. The district coordinator for traffic safety education also worked in my school. And after speaking with both of them again, I had confirmed that there was a very high demand for another instructor. And since drivers education isn't something that teachers stand in long lines for, hoping to God they get a shot at it, I figured I did have a shot at it. The hourly pay was well over twice what I was doing and the number of hours per month looked like it was going to be half again as many, although they were not concentrated in four weekends per month. Rather, they were spread out over the other days as well.

I spent the rest of the winter and spring saving what I could, working extra if it was possible, to put together enough money to not only attend the summer school certification program, but to cover lost table food money for my planned six week absence. With a little help from a tax return that spring, I managed to get myself enrolled at Central Washington University in the six week Traffic Safety Education Program.

The remainder of the winter and the spring time washing season passed somewhat quickly, due mostly to my belief that there was something beyond it. Namely, as I calculated it, it would be at least a $500 per month increase *above* what I was already bringing in from my washing job to help maintain family needs. My plan for paying off my credit card debt early was falling into place, and my belief that it could be done had never been greater.

From the Mountains Inside

I often find myself saying *somehow*. How did I ever make it through that school year? I really started wearing myself down physically. My responsibilities in the classroom were not entirely being met and I was out of gas months before June. I did get a second wind. Springtime is wonderful for that. When March first arrived, as far as I was concerned it was spring. The gray skies above the pressure washing sites didn't seem so dreary and I couldn't wait to be sitting in a classroom and behind the wheel learning my new trade. I spent most of my time during the working weekends rehearsing some new Shakespeare monologues while I scrubbed tractors. I remember specifically working on one from *Hamlet* which really wasn't good to have coursing through my mind because he was such a gloomy character. I didn't need the gloom, but the language was something I couldn't keep away from.

There remained for me the issue of where I would stay during the weeks that summer. It was a good three hour drive to Ellensburg, Washington. I had actually entertained the idea of camping because the summer dorm rooms were very expensive. I decided to put a small ad in the local newspaper looking for an apartment to sublet and it drew the attention of a retired couple in a trailer park that had a spare bedroom and private bathroom on the opposite side of their main living area. They only wanted ten dollars a night. It ended up being cheaper than camping.

They were very friendly and cleared out a small cupboard in their kitchen and a small space in their refrigerator for me to store my food items. But they smoked so much they looked like apparitions sitting in their living room. Most nights I put a damp towel at the bottom of my bedroom door to keep the smoke from wafting into my end of the house. But the manure smell from a neighboring cattle field came crashing through the window screen on the other side and roughed me up nightly. Yikes. So, I spent as much time as I could at the campus studying.

It was good for me to be a student again just to remind myself of the horrors we put kids through at times. The main professor was a real ball of fire. Holy cow, I think driftwood would have been more animated. Although he was a friendly man and one couldn't help but liking him, he had long spent his last creative notion. He was so stiff and boring; he was probably only a half a notch more exciting than a math teacher, if that gives you any idea.

It was a good summer. It had been over a year since the crash and again I was spending a large portion of time away from Julie which she still needed I'm sure. But I missed my kids horribly. I managed to see them every weekend of the six I had been gone. I went home most weekends and even got in a couple of weekends of truck washing for good measure. I was looking forward to my last day as a scrubber.

One night I was at the library studying the concept of "space management" in driving. I was reading through a three inch thick manual: The *Washington State Traffic Safety Education Curriculum Resource Guide.* Simultaneously, I was reflecting on my personal crash. And the words leapt out of the book and grabbed me by the nose. It was a section on habits and judgments, and how they can help us or get us into conflict in the traffic scene. "We often get acceptable performance feedback for unacceptable performance situations," it said. "The driver who is habitually programmed to maintain a set speed or position may not be mentally prepared to make a judgmental adjustment until the potential hazard develops to a point where it cannot be ignored. With a forced action created by ignoring the early developments of the situation, the driver is placed into a surprise situation that becomes less controllable and certainly more stressful than it needs to be."

I don't know exactly why this was so exciting to me, but perhaps it was my ability to connect the dots, and my faith in something bigger than myself that probably led me to become someone who teaches teenagers about *reducing risk.* Who else could speak about reducing risk? I would be responsible, really, for teaching them to avoid the crashes in life, by imagining that it was all about simply driving a car instead.

The section went on with "…coping with area changes rarely is difficult when a response is initiated early enough. Failing to recognize the area changes or closures, therefore delaying a corrective response, could place greater stress on the driver and the vehicle, making it more likely to exceed the limitations which could result in a failure." The *driver, vehicle,* and *failure.* Me and my life, I thought. Amen. I took it home with me and shared it with my counselor. She

91

smiled gently at me like I was on to something, finally. She didn't talk much but knew how to ask the right questions and give me the rope to hang myself. She made things come tumbling out of me like useless items out of an old closet.

We worked with Ellensburg High School Students that summer who graciously lent themselves to our first time endeavors. It was great experience and there were no close calls anywhere near the ones I was going to encounter back home. It was often artificial because from time to time we were being observed in the back seat by another teacher candidate and Professor Stiff himself. But I remember the last drive I did that summer very well. I got out of the car and said to myself, I'll never get into the car with another student again without getting paid to do it. It was big for me because another chapter of my plan was about to start rolling.

Teaching Traffic Safety as we called it turned out to be enjoyable. I was assigned a Saturday class and most days of the week after school, as well as Saturday itself to drive. I remember my first month I logged fifty one hours, and it was never less than sixty five after that. Most months it hovered above eighty hours, and this was in addition to my regular math teaching assignments. After the first semester, I had an after school class that met twice a week that was added to my Saturday responsibilities and, whammo, I was slammed with no free time. But I was making more money than I ever had in my life and I was landing some punishing blows on my debt.

Three weeks after I started, I had a girl make a right hand turn in what I thought was a low volume neighborhood. She swung out too wide into the lane of an oncoming truck coming up over the crest of a hill. I grabbed the wheel and yanked it to the right, while she panicked and stomped on the accelerator. We hell-drove across some lady's driveway and then outstripped the wind across her yard and came to a stop four inches from a lovely pine tree. It was surrounded with a raised bed of flowers. We always had a dual brake in the vehicle, of course, and I was surprised I didn't stomp a hole through to the earth's mantle trying to keep us from totaling the car. It was a 1999 Chevy Lumina. A pretty dark blue with a now new, but small set of scuff marks near the front bumper. The resident came out of her house with a cell phone stuck in one ear, and her mouth dragging on her front steps. She was very forgiving, thankfully. She was very concerned about the kid behind the wheel.

The student began crying and I was rattled, thinking that there could've been a toddler in the yard. What would have I done then? I started to wonder what I got myself into. Then another girl in the back seat pipes up, "It's okay, *anybody* could've done it!" Not what I was thinking even remotely. My boss told me to relax, that the scuffs could be buffed out and that another incident was not likely to happen to me for another thirty years. Unfortunately, he was only twenty nine years, eleven months and one week off. And it occurred with the same student.

This one was good. We pulled into the parking lot of the high school and she turned into one of the angle parking spaces across a very short distance from the front doors. Many students enjoyed this feeling of coming back into the parking lot. There were usually many other students waiting out front and they felt a certain pride, I guess, with driving in front of their peers. This girl thinks she's applying the brake as she gets settled into the space, but again goes postal on me with the accelerator. I was ready for it though, sort of.

The car goes lunging forward over the curb into some beach rock and the tires start a ripping, vicious attack on the landscaping, and she still has it gunned down to the floor. I respond with a lightning quick counter attack on my dual brake. It was like the sympathetic and the parasympathetic nervous systems kicked in high mode at the same time (I also learned this from my psychology degree). We were locked in a dual, the accelerator versus the brake. She was winning however because the car was slowly advancing toward a busy street just feet away by short, loud, lurching bursts. She was locked into a confused, unresponsive state as she ignored my pleas to let off the gas. The engine roared and the front wheel drive tore buckets and buckets of beach rock out of the landscaping and sent it hurtling across the parking lot behind the car and directly to the front of the school and peppered the front doors like bullets. Boyfriends and girlfriends lost in the presence of adolescence and each other suddenly found themselves dodging rock and dirt that was slamming into the door. They were skipping and hopping from one foot to the next, and diving out of the way. It looked like a tap dance break from *42nd Street* combined with a drive-by shooting.

This particular car was the 1999 Chevy Lumina. You know, it was a pretty dark blue with a new but small set of scuff marks near the front bumper. When it was all over, more than half it was up over the curb and in the brush of the landscaping, and the parking sign, *This space reserved for the principal,* was flattened. That wasn't a problem. We parked there all the time after school hours. She didn't cry this time. She elected to remain in the car and slunk down in the seat as if she was looking for the fuse box. The front tires of the car were buried so far up that the car was almost high centered on the landscaping curb.

Now I figured that no incidents would happen again for thirty years. And although I had been on many people's lawns after this, you know, trying to street park and all, nothing nearly as critical happened afterward. At least as far as drivers education was concerned. Although I did have to take a knife away from a student once during an after school class at our district's other high school. That was delightful. I think his punishment was *two* nights to bed early, so that he would be sure to never do *that* again. Most of the incidents involved tires rolling up the curb by lawns and then over one or two feet of grass, nothing serious.

But some really isolated, bizarre events occurred as well. Making a left hand turn one winter in a residential neighborhood, this student didn't feel the need to steer the entire ninety degrees to make the turn. No, she figured forty five degrees was about enough and was headed straight for a fire hydrant after straightening the tires out. Not a problem for most kids, they would see that it wasn't enough and adjust. But this particular kid didn't see anything wrong whatsoever with what she was targeting! She was mildly annoyed that I mentioned she was heading for a collision, and more annoyed that I actually grabbed her steering wheel to avoid it when she didn't respond! She couldn't tell that she was headed for trouble.

Three years of this went by very quickly. I made the kids listen to some of my Shakespeare monologues while they drove because the radio was strictly forbidden in my car. I also threatened to make all occupants of the vehicle wear helmets. I figured if it was good enough for motorcyclists, it was good enough for Mr. Powell and the gang, what with all the massive head injuries that are common in serious car collisions. I actually had one kid who said he wouldn't object as long as I would drop him off four miles from the front of the high school. I could never figure out what was so traumatic about pulling into the high school parking lot with helmets on. Oh well.

I was fond of pulling in traffic safety examples into my eighth grade math classes. These kids would soon be driving with me, after all, so I thought I would get a leg up on the situation by simulating some lane changing techniques or space management skills in class. I even tried to apply these things to hallway behavior. I figured if they kept a good following distance and maintained a good visual lead time, they would cut down on their tardies. I thought it was brilliant, you know, but...kids these days, what can I say?

As the months passed, teaching became more enjoyable. My life had variety and I was more willing to draw on my own experiences than I was in the past. Helping kids to see possible trouble and adjust to it before things become critical had a certain appeal to me, even more so because I was teaching them to do so while trying to redeem myself from my own disaster. At the end of the first two years though, I was working so much that I ended up getting sick. I missed a week and a half of school about three weeks before the summer break contending with pneumonia. Eighty five hours a month, month in and month out, along with trying to stay above water at the middle school was too much. I taught about a thousand hours of traffic safety that school year, including the summer break, and everything was catching up to me.

I remember it hit me right before lunch. I was slammed with the shivers. I was so cold I had to put on my king costume with the wool cape. There wasn't a substitute immediately available so I had to wait one more period after lunch before she arrived. I went in my classroom, told the kids I was sick, put my head down on my desk and let them run the show while I convulsed and muttered with the chills in my own corner of the room. They were unequivocally in charge and unsupervised. They could've cared less if I'd have dropped unconscious on the floor. Apparently the urgency of my situation had no potential to penetrate their world, because one kid came up to me and said, "Mr. Powell, I'm bored, and the room is very loud and you don't seem to be listening to me." I think I just pulled my face up slightly out of my own slobber and lifted one eyelid open far enough to moan. That's it. That's all I had the energy for.

I had to drive myself home and I stayed there for a week and a half. I was useless to my family and I was ineffective in getting decent plans to my substitute teacher. I remember thinking one day at home if I could have, I would've called 911 for an ambulance because of a particularly nasty episode of a raging fever. I started to hallucinate and I blacked out. Julie came home from a bike ride and found me writhing around on the floor. I really should have gone to the hospital, but instead I settled for an outpatient treatment. The first round of antibiotics had no effect, which scared me. After they were switched, I began to heal up. A hundred years ago, I would've been dead.

Traffic safety was fun. I worked many, many hours alongside my friend Mike Fosburg. We had many Saturday lunches together and traveled to two traffic safety conferences together. It made it much easier that we were teachers in the same middle school building, as well as having the district coordinator of traffic safety in our building. Mike actually taught a math class in my room when I was on my prep period, so we communicated a lot. At the high school, I drove with his students some times, and he drove with mine. I covered his classes, he covered mine. We made a great team. He became a great confidant, and was very encouraging in my quest. He did more for me than I will realize, and I know he did more for me than he realizes. God bless Mike Fosburg.

The attraction to teaching drivers education was the reality and applicability of it. Many people would say that the kids would all be motivated to show up and learn, and remain focused. This was generally true, but there were still plenty of students in the mix who couldn't handle following the rules and felt as if a drivers license was something bestowed upon them as a birthright when they came of age. These kids were a scream. It was an absolute pleasure to watch them struggle with natural consequences knowing that someday they would get it. Just as I was "getting it", albeit later in life.

One particular winter over Christmas break, Mike and I had the kids out one very snowy Saturday afternoon in the high school parking lot. Naturally it was empty, but it was covered with eight inches of fresh snow. We thought we would show the kids what it was like to be behind the wheel of a vehicle that was out of control. We had them accelerate and slam the brakes and try to steer out of imaginary trouble. It was fun for them to be doing donuts in the high school parking lot. Although had Mike and I thought it through, we might have scheduled ourselves to be in the parking lot at different times, if you know what I'm getting at.

I don't know how often we raced by one another, but it would have been very embarrassing for two drivers education teachers to slam their two district leased, student-loaded cars together in the deep snow in an empty parking lot. Countless times I flew by him sideways, and he certainly slipped past me close enough to do a high five. I think once we skidded backward past each other. Later, after we talked it through and decided not to do that again at the same time, we laughed out loud very hard at what could've happened. (But I have never in my life seen anyone laugh so hard for such a long time as when Mike watched me eat what I *thought* were crunchy artichoke hearts in my calzone at lunch one time. They turned out to be cloves of garlic...all sixteen of them. I think the cook was a former student of ours. Mike cried he was laughing so hard.)

The kids learned what it felt like to be out of control, at least in a car, and although it was tremendous fun for them, they admitted that they had no idea it could be such a helpless feeling. Real life physics, I love it. They also learned that the world is not always going to be friendly. The "Student Driver" sign hanging out of the back of the trunk is supposed to encourage cooperation from the rest of the roadway users, but it was an invitation to intimidate to others. They often got honked at, flipped off and cursed at. It is a powerful experience for the teacher to have no control over the rest of the world, to teach them about it without shielding them from it. "What do you want me to do?" I would ask them, "Call their parents? Give them detention? *This* is what you have to learn to manage. You have to learn how to interact successfully with other users." They wanted independence, but they were often overcome with a tremendous sense of injustice. I always reminded them that they were on a mission to become adults, but also reminded them often that I wasn't going to hold their hands all the way there and steal part of the process from them. (Constructivist teachers would've loved me saying this.) "You make the decisions" I would say, "You have to develop the ability to think your way through it."

They would ask me, "What's the speed limit here?"

"What do you think?" I would reply. "It's not always going to be readily noticeable, so look around and get some clues and make your decision. How many lanes are on this street? How fast is the other traffic flowing? Is it a business area or residential area? What condition do you think the roadway is in now? I'm not always going to be around to answer these questions for you."

Other times we would find ourselves blocked in behind some oversized vehicle at a traffic light, and other vehicles squeezed in all around us. I was in such a situation with a car load of girls one time and the reality of the world was ever present on the oversized bumper sticker that was directly in front of us, right about eyeball level. There was absolutely no way anyone could miss this one. An oversized bumper sticker, with oversized bold lettering. "Show Me Your Tits" it read. It did no good for me to look to the right or the left, nothing remained for me to become distracted by. Defeated, I simply stared straight forward. And of course the light was going to be an especially long wait that time. At last, one of the girls in the back seat cuts into the silence and blurts out, "Kinda makes ya feel uncomfortable, doesn't it Mr. Powell!" You can bet we made a quick lane change around that fella when we had the chance, you betcha.

Every once in awhile, we would pass a truck on the road that I used to wash. Or we would sit next to one at a traffic light. I would sit there and reflect, remembering the uncertainty of that first year, and how invigorating it could be to wash. But also the dreariness as the months passed into winter, and the decision I made that one winter night to change that put me on this particular path. I was learning how important it is to have a clear line of sight and a clear travel path, two important things to establish in your driving practice. I never forgot the importance of that first year.

Julie asked me once if I was going to miss washing trucks, and as smelly and dreary as it could be, most of the time it wasn't. I said yes, I was going to miss it mostly because it gave me another chance to think things through. I did end up missing it somewhat because it had a poetic quality about it that made me a better teacher in the end. However, nothing beat drivers education. I *never* would have went in to it if I didn't need the money, but once I was there I discovered it had more in store for me than I imagined. I felt a sense of achievement bringing myself up to sitting in the instructor's seat of a car from that life changing winter night washing trucks.

Three years of Traffic Safety Education turned out to be enough. The district had elected to eliminate the program due to rising costs so Mike and I finished our last school year and last summer school session. Ironically, it was the same summer that I had eliminated my credit card debt. I had whipped it. It was much more profitable than washing trucks. I had brought home generally three times the amount I was making on the wash jobs, and every extra penny of it was going to my creditors. At the end of every month, I put a check in the mail and took a forceful swing at an imaginary opponent. It was going down. I had felt this long before because I was going for its heart. I had paid it off two years early. Oddly, this may have been the greatest personal achievement in my life.

In fact, four years after my crash, Julie and I had no credit debt. We had no car loans, no computer loans, no other consumer loans at all except a final student loan that I paid off a year later. So in a way, traffic safety was like Mary Poppins, coming in long enough to get things turned around and then left. I was infinitely grateful for the opportunity to work hard at something worth teaching and equally thankful for the opportunity to learn something myself. Our little house was for sale, and Julie and I were preparing to move into a dream home where we could keep our horses (previously boarded), enjoy a large yard and garden, have lots of room for the kids to grow, and move into the next phase of our life together.

Currently the only debt Julie and I have is our house payment, and we currently save about one third of our net income every month for cash reserve, college education, family vacations and automobiles. Two years after the debt was eradicated, we bought a newer truck with cash. Everyone makes car payments. We just decided to make the payments to ourselves, which we continue to do every month. When it's time for a new vehicle, we go out and buy it. It's not always easy at first. It takes time to get the traction on this strategy and contend with life's little surprises at the same time. But it works. *Good things take time.* Some of my friends asked me how we got out of the mess so quickly, and I say it's because of two reasons: We're smart and we're disciplined. And it's just as easy to be smart as it is to be disciplined.

We also had a powerful force behind us, especially me. When you're rafting down a wild river, it isn't just the immediate forces around you that are influencing you. It is the entire force of all the water in the mountains behind you that are really forcing a change. It is the sum of all these forces. And so it was with me; I drew my power from the mountains inside.

However unnecessary and painful it was for me to choose the path that I had just completed, I hold a certain fondness for having been through it. Understand, I am *not* interested in traveling through it all again, nor do I wish it on anyone else. But I am certain that I am stronger for it.

Shakespeare wrote "They say best men are molded out of faults, and, for the most, become much more the better for being a little bad." And I often wonder, how much is a *little* bad?

The Parent Company

Every summer we teachers experience teacher dreams. Well, for me they're often in the summer anyway, but I know teachers have them from time to time. Usually they revolve around a repeating theme of being unprepared, anxiety, and general incoherency. But one of the last ones I had was slightly different. A plot unfolded regarding my kidnapping by a militant group of parents. The militant group of parents actually existed, but in my dream they kidnapped me, threatened me, and kept me from my family. This is how I came to relate to them as the parent mafia.

Imagine a Brando-esque, Godfather voice, "This is my son's teacher Mr. Powell. He's always talkin' when he should be listenin'." But the thing I couldn't get over in my dream was that they didn't throw me into a limo, it wasn't a Cadillac or any other big luxury vehicle. They grabbed me off the street and tossed me into a Volkswagen bus! A Volkswagen! This may have been the most disturbing thought of all. For the life of me, I couldn't make sense out of this. In my dream, I don't remember what they told me, but I do remember a lot of finger pointing in my face, and threats of "Now we wouldn't want to have this happen, now would we?" It was all done behind mirrored Foster Grants and in scruffy voices and all. Bunch of wanna-be social hitmen defending their particular social strata.

Sometimes God plays cruel tricks on teachers and puts together the wrong combination of parents into the wrong place at the wrong time. I'm not sure you really understand me, these are the type of people who live vicariously through their children and anything interpreted by these neurotics as a slight on their children, is by golly a damn well bigger slight on them. They act like fourteen year-olds whose little brother was looked at wrongly by the unsuspecting new kid on the block, and it's then that someone is in for a fanny whoopin'.

Imagine for a moment that something new or different is offered up for a school. It could be anything from a new lunch menu item, or a new principal, to a new set of books, a new school itself or even a new class offering for kids. The only thing that matters is that it is new. For some reason it sets off this power struggle. Just like in Iraq, as soon as the new door opens a crack, every special interest group from miles around gets a whiff of the small drops of innocence and naivety, and they start circling in the waters. Opportunists suddenly appear. Arrogance seeps out and idealogues start wanting to take over. They are constantly on the lookout for a market to corner, an outpost to commandeer, and teachers to get on the payroll. Anytime something is ready for the pickin', they show up with their Foster Grants and a parking lot full of Hummers.

These people really get on my nerves. They are egotistical and boorish. They give me the weebie geebies even if they are not yet poised to pounce. Every once in awhile, I can walk to my car after school and see one of them in my periphery parked nearby hiding behind a newspaper they're pretending to read, ready to follow me to find out where I live.

"My child is gifted," is a common stake many of them may lay claim to. "We want to know what you're going to do about it." It's bizarre, they think I'm Miracle Max or something. My first action would normally be to procure them a list of home school networks in the area, but the PC Administravia Protectorship would never approve. They certainly don't need me, that's for sure. Parents who boast about their kid being gifted think that a math teacher who dresses like Shakespeare must be exactly what their kid needs, but oh dear God are they mistaken. They don't need me, and they usually realize it when they find out I don't fly through page after page and chapter after chapter and book after book. Few things render me numb like parents who think that whoever gets through the math book first are the smartest. To them it has nothing to do with development, depth, patience, immersion, versatility, flexibility, creativity or thought. It is speed, and speed alone that separates their kids from your little hayseeds. Make no mistake about it, these people are out there. And every once in a great while they find me, and end up barking up the wrong tree, convinced their personal animal is up there somewhere.

Sometimes they remind me of Prince Charles and his stupid polo games. He bounces around with a bunch of other pasty faces thinking that the rest of the world wishes they could be just like them, not understanding that we wonder instead what it's like not to have a life. And these parents, I imagine, think that all their neighbors are very envious of them for being prominent and righteous. Righteous my butt. They are usually a bunch of elitists and very much unappreciated by me. When they come to me, they don't realize that they showed up at a fine Italian restaurant trying to order Kentucky Fried Chicken, and I end up having to tell them that it's not on the menu.

Sometimes parents are slow to get this. They seem convinced that they understand my madness and think it's great, and they give you the line about it being important "to have good math teachers like you". But once they're in, and it's been a couple of weeks, the first highly predictable comment comes rolling in.

"Johnny is bored, and he's not being challenged."

And I flash back, "Excuse me? He's earning himself a D. I'd say he has plenty of challenge on his plate."

But what the hell do I know, I mean don't forget the jack ass they're talking to, right? He can't *possibly* be serious. We need to fix him. It's like in *Guys and Dolls* when Sky Masterson says that as soon as a dame finds the right guy to marry, she marches him right in after the wedding for alterations. It is a scream. When Johnny has a D, it's because he's not being challenged and he's bored and he's a genius. No other factors remain that are even remotely related. These people are a piece of work because you don't get that way overnight.

It's somewhat amusing to watch the Protectorship interact with these people. They try so hard with all the talk of "accommodation" and "meeting the needs" and all, they forget that they may sound more like an appeaser. The PC Administravia Protectorship of the Appeasement. Winston Churchill said that appeasers are the people who throw chickens to the crocodiles in the hopes that they will be the last people eaten. It's similar to abusive boyfriends in relationships. The *absolute soonest* you can cut them out of the girl's life the easier it will be. If you let it drag on, you're in for trouble. Didn't Leonardo da Vinci also say something about things being easier to resist at the beginning than at the end? I'm sure he did. Anyway, what the hell do Churchill and da Vinci know? They're just a couple of white males anyway.

Yes, it is my belief they can be abusive, even though it really only ends up being a small handful of them wherever they show up across America. It's the kids that end up on the short end anyway. But like I always say, how many drops of strychnine does it take to completely poison a cup of tea? Huh? I thought so.

Remember in Shakespeare's *Titus Andronicus* when Titus is so attached to the ways of the Roman Empire that when one of his sons questions this, Titus runs a dagger through him? Same thing. Sort of. Well, never mind, just forget that example.

Let's imagine being gum under the table at a first time parent meeting in a brand new school. We listen in as they might discuss whether they should be a P.T.A. or a P.T.O. I wouldn't even know there was a difference until after the parents broke out into a shouting session. I would only be perhaps a distant ear witness to this though, and as far as I might be able to tell, they may sound like dogs at the pound: each one trying to get in the loudest bark as possible in the interest of establishing a pecking order.

Sometimes adults are absolutely no different than eleven year-olds, in many cases worse. I recommend that you go to a middle school sporting event and watch the etiquette that some parents show up with. It is truly an eye opening experience. But you have to go with the intention of being an unbiased observer. Being at these events and the issue of their kid winning at all costs is as urgent and life threatening to these people as an emergency 911 call for massive head injury.

Every now and then I imagine being in charge at a school and see the parental tsunami on the horizon. I would tell them to butt out and back off as soon as I got a whiff of their true smell, which would probably be three weeks before school even started. They wouldn't be coming in to my school making demands. They're just like a school bully. You start getting harassed, you let him know that if he keeps it up, a drubbing will follow. When it happens again, *immediately* pop him in the nose, wait no more than two seconds for him to figure out what happened, but not really, then *do it again.* Disable the bastard. End of problem. This works because bullies never expect this to happen. *That's how bullies get this way in the first place!! Am I making any sense to anybody out there!* Yeah, yeah, I know what you're thinking. How could a teacher say this? Well, read it again and see. I'm not the only one out here that's sick of these people. They're almost as bad as Texas cheerleader parents.

Yeah, yeah, yeah I know I probably wouldn't last being in charge of a school anyway. I'm not PC enough. Okay, good point. But here's another good point: the administration is supposed to work *with* the parents, not *for* the parents. For some parents (and for some administrators too, I suppose) letting go of some control makes the ego flaccid.

It might be a true educational experience to watch a bunch of these parents light some torches and set out with their hounds looking for Frankenstein's monster. Inevitably, somewhere along the line they will lose the scent and wind up chasing down some fifth grade teachers instead. Of course, these teachers have to go, they will contend. They will end up confronting the school board in some fashion by crashing into the meeting with some teachers roped up and soaked in kerosene.

For these poor, misdirected folks there is *always* some issue, some concern, some meeting that has to be conducted, some conflict that has to be addressed, a conference to settle this, and a time where "we could meet to change that." They remind me of a character in a Stephen King novel, *Needful Things* I think. Her name was Vera, or Nora or something like that. Vera in a red rage was Vera fulfilled, he wrote, imbued with high purpose. Stephen King must have been a teacher at one time. Can you imagine Stephen King writing a novel about a school in New England that has somehow reached the end of its rope with the parents? They start disappearing one by one, and the school board members become the victims of a mysterious haunting characterized by the screaming presences of Jacob Marley type vaporizations. I can't do it justice. It just needs to be turned over to Stephen King himself, that's all.

I had another dream one night when I worked at another school. I dreamt that I showed up on the first day of school and it was snowing a very wet, sloppy, slushy snow. And I got out of my car and had no shoes on. I was barefoot and my arms were loaded with books and materials, and again, I had no lesson plans. (No lesson plans is a repeating motif in teachers' dreams.) I was thoroughly unprepared for this day. I made my way to the front door of the school. I shuffled helplessly through the parking lot while my feet burned in the cold slush. As fate would have it the door was locked. I yanked on it with a tremendous amount of effort with a free pinky, and no one would help me. Other teachers peered at me from the inside, wanting to help but knowing the consequences if they did. Suddenly a crowd of parents began forming around me and besieged me with snowballs. They came from all sides, and beaned me in the back and in the head. Then they broke off enormous melting icicles from the low roof line and clubbed me into a bloody unconsciousness.

It was very much like something out of the Old Testament or Ancient Rome, or a Kate Jackson short story, or even a Martin Scorsese film. Actually when I awoke from the dream, it reminded me of some of the battle scenes in Macbeth or Henry V, except those were one team versus another team and my "team" decided to stay inside the foyer of the locked front door and treat it like a side show. There could've been blood stained snow spattered around the door and in the distance the kids could've gathered in groups to surmise the incident before shrugging it off as another existentialist blip. The parents wouldn't blink. They would be like reptiles and just stare vacuously past the faces around them, and their heart rates would not have risen in the slightest. Yikes, where am I going with this one?

Later on that year when school began in reality, I connected this incident to the function $y = 1/x$. If you know how to graph this function or know what it looks like, you'll see that as the x values increase, the y values decrease (at least in quadrant I). I always call these functions of decay because if the x-axis represents time, and the y-axis represents something like Mr. Powell's survivability coefficient, his survivability decays over time. So I saw myself represented in that dream by this particular function. Real life math.

Yes, I am okay. Although I have been accused of being sick in the head many times, by students anyway. I had a girl one time whose mom had a private practice as a family counselor and the kid kept pestering her to make some room in her schedule to sneak an appointment in for me. What could I say? The kid was looking out for me.

Of course, parents aren't always sinister monsters. The vast majority are quite the opposite actually. They're just quiet and very supportive in a very covert way. I'm not sure, but I think in one school, they met secretly to pray for my recovery from insanity. In fact this category is the one the vast majority of them fall in to. Not insanity, but quiet and supportive. If they ever decided to organize and rise up against the evil other end, you would find more teachers willing to take a pay cut and standardized test scores would start swelling. Well, I don't know. I'm not sure about that. Maybe they will rise up someday, though it seems most people don't against bullies. Sometimes I get the feeling that ninety percent of us are happy saying nothing at all, even when we know we are right. Why is that?

I use this form note to send home to parents of kids missing assignments. I write in a somewhat broken Shakespearean language, and I include many references to the Bard's use of "peevish schoolboys" and "creeping like snail unwillingly to school". I always ended them with a comment about parents and teachers working together: We will tell your young student to rest assured that "we come to speak with our hands and not our tongues", and "talkers are no good doers". I sent one home one time in the winter, and the father sent the following back to me:

Mr. Powell~

In the fortnight prior to the recently passed holiday season, you kindly advised us of a couplet of homework assignments that had not yet been delivered on their hour at the hands of young Bobby.. As of the date herewith, and with repeated, albeit gentle prodding on my part, young Bobby has

*yet to supply us with any further information as to
the missing assignments...*

I was charmed already. I had dropped everything I
was doing that morning and basked in the glory of gaining
another parental ally. The kid sat at his table grumpy and
defeated because he was getting a lashing of Shakespearean
proportions from both flanks: home and school. He
concludes:

*...Alas Mr. Powell, we are not wont to visit an
inglorious winter of discontent upon young Bobby's
head. I rather suspect that after learning the
nature of our communication he will consider his
gluteus maximus summarily, if not succinctly well
booted. As always, the fault is not in our stars but
in ourselves.*

Keep up the good work.

As victorious as this was for me, somehow young
Bobby knew that my hands were going to be much too busy
with the parent brute squad to lean on him in an effective,
consistent way. So his dad and I corresponded a few more
times for refresher attempts.

Conference time is a treat. I think there should be
public viewing rooms for taxpayers to come in and watch
one of these take place. At the schools I've been in, we've
had conferences that were led, or supposed to be led by
students. The kid does all the talking, the kid talks about
his strengths and weaknesses, he shows what he is learning,
and he exhibits several examples of his work. Unless the
kid is still not potty trained. Then he sits there slumped
over with the mouth hanging wide open and a little bit of

dribble doing that yo-yo thing off the bottom lip. Couldn't get a ripple on an EEG. These can be absolutely agonizing, but not as agonizing as the ones with the single mom sitting there, exhausted from trying her heart out. And her kid slouches next to her and actually has the balls to roll his eyes at her, and mock her attempts to motivate her little drugged up pin head. The kid needed popped in the face a couple of times. I have no patience for this. I felt so bad for the mom I stopped the conference, stepped in and told the kid to sit up and show some respect to his own mother, or we could continually start the conference over from the beginning several times if we needed to in order to get this right.

Anyway, parents are really there to help and they can be tremendous fun. I once had a parent who knew I was a Shakespearean, and quizzed me during his daughter's conference on several lines from some of the plays. For example, he would say "Let Hercules himself do what he may…" and I would reply, "…the cat will mew and dog will have his day." He had me sweating there for a few minutes but I managed to get most of the quotes finished off. This of course had to be done to the chagrin of the kid and her mom who were sitting nearby wondering whose conference this really was anyway. He told me I didn't do badly for a math teacher. I was pleased.

Christmas is a time where many parents send gifts in, and the kids too. I have been amazed at some of the gifts that have come across my desk. Flowers, candy, pencils, mugs, CDs, the Book of Mormon, cookies, ties, and calendars to name a few. We get cards and gift certificates and refrigerator magnetic poetry kits. One year I had two students get me the same Shakespeare magnetic poetry kit so I used one at home and one at school.

The one I used at home my kids got into and found out that they could put their own Shakespearean phrases together. This was very engaging for them, even at six and eight years of age. I figured it was rubbing off on them when one day my six year-old son started racing me to the car and yelled, "Dad, last one to the car's a loathsome scab!"

One parent actually put a $45 copy of the *Complete Works of William Shakespeare* under my Christmas tree. She went on about how I was her son's favorite teacher and how he absolutely loved my class, but he always sat there in class like a lab mouse staring down a python. He looked like he would rather be anywhere but stuck in my freak show classroom. I really could never, never figure these particular kids out.

I developed relationships with parents over the years simply by seeing them after school. They would just stop in to see how *I* was doing. Imagine that. There was a mom several years ago who stopped in, looked at me, and immediately asked me if my kidneys had dropped. I really wasn't sure how to respond, but what she really meant, I guess, was that I didn't look so healthy. She immediately set her purse aside, approached me and put her hands on the side of my neck feeling for lumps or swollen something or others, and shook her head from side to side as if she arrived a little too late. Then she pulled a few items out of her purse and started "muscle testing" me. Apparently, she would touch these vials of strange substances to my body, have me try to counter the resistance of her hand putting pressure on my arm, and be able to tell something about my internal organs. I later found out it had something to do with applied kinesiology.

She attached blame for my condition to her son and immediately whisked him out of school and kept him at home for a couple of days until I got the color back in my face. Man, I don't know what the deal was there but she was a kind woman. If I'd have known my kidneys had slooped or dropped or whatever, I might not have come into school that day. But I went home and had a bowl of Lucky Charms and a beer and I was right back with it, after of course her son was away for the two days.

I discovered after some time too, that parents and other adults could be trained just like the kids. Being adults, they just needed more Mr. Powell exposure time I guess. I got this idea one time to dress myself up like the Pope during progress report time. The kids received their current grades for the term to take home and get signed by Mom and Dad. I always had them come up to my desk and we would have a sixty second review of their productivity so far. And there I was in a sky blue robe with a white bishop-looking hat I made out of butcher paper and a napkin holder. Well, it turned out that day that the kids were especially respectful to me, almost reverent I would say.

And also as it turned out, there were a couple of parents visiting and skipped their way up to my room for a quick look at the wack job Mr. Powell. One mom actually grabbed my hand, the one with the two big rings on it, and kissed it. The kids, simply stared at me, quietly, for a very long time. But she knew the game and had been around and felt comfortable enough to jump right in and play along, just like the kids do.

I got myself in trouble with the Pope costume though because some ignoramus said that it was unconstitutional because of the "separation of church and state" thing that is supposed to be in the U.S. Constitution. Which it isn't by the way. But the PC Protectorship would do whatever it took to avoid a showdown. Personally, I thought my white trash costume that one Halloween was worse.

The members of the PC Administravia Protectorship were the only ones whoever said anything. The parents all thought it was great, but it sure gets the administrators wringing their hands. It's just like at Christmas time. I was in a school one time where we were not to say the word "Christmas" because it was going to be offensive to the other .00000472 % of the kids and families in the school. We could, however, say "Happy Hanukkah" or "Rah Rah for Ramadan!" But anything Christmas was right out. It seemed so blatantly stupid that I almost stayed home for a couple of days. Where were the parents on this one? Most of them came from a Christian background; that's *the way America is!* But the real kicker is that on the night of the "Winter Program" our choir kids got up there and sang *Silent Night,* and nobody says a word. It utterly staggers the imagination.

It's amazing how many kids are like their parents. We've all heard the "apple from the tree" line. But what I have found out is there can be some very interesting dynamics between parents and their children. Subtle, sometimes subconscious manipulation games going back and forth, initiated on both sides. It's very fascinating to watch. It's also fun when you get a smart ass kid who shows up at a conference with his smart ass dad. The two cocky schmedricks just sit there at the table across from you and they banter back and forth with their trademark smart assery, just going at each other, wondering why the dumb ass is being a dumb ass in school. Until they both decide that it's Mr. Powell's fault for not contacting "Dad" soon enough.

This of course takes place in front of the mom who sits passively in the back trying to smile through it all and wondering how she got mixed up with these two jerks in the first place. When it is her time to talk, she feels compelled to agree that it is indeed Mr. Powell's fault, but you can tell that she's paying lip service to the boys. The session ends with dear old dad throwing his business card down in front of me, like he's in one of those old tough-guy-Steve McQueen movies dealing a poker hand to citizens of ill-repute. If it wasn't a school, he would've had a cigarette flipping up and down from his lips while he tried to squint like Clint Eastwood giving an icy stare to the guy everybody knows is a crook except the mayor and the Chief of Police. When he left the parking lot that day, he probably drove like Steve McQueen too. That s.o.b. Powell.

There are plenty of times when we adults simply do not get it. Many years ago I had this little seventh grade girl in pre-algebra. She spent two or three days a week doing nothing but sobbing her eyes out in my class the entire period, sometimes more. She wasn't disruptive; she simply put her head down and tried to be quiet about it. I couldn't take it any longer. I tried to talk to her about it with no success. She didn't do any work and she didn't seem to be improving. I consulted one of our counselors and found out three days later that her parents were going through a very intense and bitter divorce. And of course this beautiful kid was the focal point of some heated arguing. But they were not arguing over who *got* to keep her. Did you read that correctly? I'll say it again, and you connect the dots. They were not arguing over who *got* to keep her. It's delightful when a kid gets everything she needs like this, isn't it? Chapter one of *How to Make a Child Fail* begins right there. Fortunately, there are kids out there who are writing chapter one of *How to Succeed Despite Your Parents.*

There are still other kids that are at the mercy of us clueless adults. I was standing in a conference session regarding a young seventh grade boy who was failing classes, not participating, demonstrating behaviors indicative of depression and not dressing down for P.E. At first glance, it looked as if the kid was just doing all of this out of spite. His dad was just exasperated. This kid was not present as I was in the room with the parent, intervention specialists, counselors and other teachers, our vice principal and maybe one other social worker. (Are not we all social workers?) If you'd have known the boy, you could see that there was something else going on. His standardized test scores were solid and his past teachers reported no problems.

But middle school is the time when kids start discovering other things about themselves, and things they may already be aware of are become more glaring, hint, hint. It wasn't until the father huffed that "I don't know why he won't dress down in P.E., he loves P.E., he dances five days a week for crying out loud," that something turned inside of me. It wasn't until I heard the disgust in the man's voice, combined with the fact that he was not dressing down, combined with the dancing, combined with the kid's overabundance of friends that were girls, that I realized that the kid was gay.

And how frustrating it was for me to stand in a room with all these professionals wringing their hands and scratching their heads, *knowing* what the issue was but not being able to breathe one word about it that can really make a guy feel useless. Can you imagine if I would've been asked for my honest opinion about it? In a room swishing with the paper-shuffling of PC Administravia? It would've fallen completely silent except for the sound of pee running down everyone's pants and on to the floor.

I have been called a Godsend by one set of parents and "that horrible, horrible man" by others. What can I say? I guess some of them don't like me. Every once in a great while, I find myself sitting in the office for a conference with a parent or two about the how-dare-I-raise-my-voice deal. But get this, I've also found myself thrown in there for the exact opposite reason! Too much emotional reality versus not enough. One thing among ten thousand that they don't teach you in graduate school is that there is a certain caste of parent who is entirely behind your system of accountability unless, of course, it involves his own kid. It's then that you've burned a little too much rubber. And then I discovered that some of these parents are teachers themselves. Believe me, teachers do not unite on every issue. That's why I call teaching an art and not a science. We deal with over-developed sensitivities one minute, and barbarians the next. The best strategy I've discovered during the office talks is to stare out the window and reaffirm to myself that I will soon be back in the classroom with the kids. They end up being much more flexible and resilient than the adults anyway.

No wonder I get numb and stupid from teaching school. It's no mystery why I'm searching for some other stimuli to get me through my life. Why don't you do something else, you may then ask. That's usually a question that brand new teachers, and others who know no better would ask. But, perhaps they are right. Every fall I come back and on the what-did-we-do-on-our-summer-break-speech I tell the staff I almost got that job of starting and stopping the ferris wheels for the traveling carnival. And though I didn't get it this time, I moved up higher on the waiting list.

They don't understand that it's not the kids; these people will never understand that it's not the kids. It's never the kids. It never was the kids. It's the adults, like clueless teachers and administrators and parents and legislators and attorneys. I could actually do a dissertation on it and they would still repeat the same old talk, fired at me repetitively like a machine gun. I'm not saying I'm more superior to them, nor am I claiming to be smarter. But you know, I can be right a lot of times too. What I am saying is, they can drive me absolutely slobberingly bonkers. They can make a train take a dirt road.

Actually, I asked my wife that question one time, or something like it. I asked my wife why I didn't become someone else, why I didn't work for a corporation. She replied, "Because they wouldn't have you." Oh yeah, I forgot. It is me. *Dump the Shakespeare, Powell. Dump the tool belt and start connecting with kids. You just don't care about kids, Powell. That's the real problem.*

I was sitting in my vice principal's office one time during my first year of teaching. I think it was about three weeks into the school year. I was waiting in there with one of those moms who can't be pleased with anything. She was desperate for a meeting. She was like an emotionally unstable, tantrum-throwing toddler who can't see past her own little world, and I do mean little. You should see moms like this get together in the parking lot after school. They're like braying mules.

Anyway, we were both waiting for the vice principal because he had a phone call or something. And it was silent, and neither one of us was looking at the other. I know she didn't like me because her daughter told me so in front of the entire class. And the crowd she hung around with hunted the halls of our school in the mornings before classes began, looking for girls to intimidate. It was Pre-Menstrual Penny and the Bitch Patrol.

So while this lovely mother and I were waiting, she decides to break the silence. "My husband and I have decided that you are the worst teacher my daughter ever had." Three weeks in to my first job, I felt compelled to reply.

First, I belched real loud, hopped up on to the chair and started beating on my chest. Then I started in.

"Yeah, well if I didn't think you were such a sour faced saucy-tongued wench, and if your daughter didn't dress like a harlot from a Tijuana cathouse, there's a possibility that I would only let you off with a defiant, 'Buzz off'. By the way, I've never seen you with a husband. I think you're making it up. If in fact you are married, with a daughter like yours, it doesn't surprise me that he's somewhere else."

Then I ripped off another belch that was so loud and resonant, I sounded like a silverback mountain gorilla. I jumped up and down three times waving my arms above my head, and then walked out on my knuckles.

I don't remember what I said. Maybe it was a politically correct smile and a couple of re-affirming nods, and a look of genuine concern, and a how-can-I-completely-change-my-personality-and-my-value-system-just-for-you-look that swept across my face as I dropped to my knees and massaged her toes. No parents who ever think a teacher is doing a great job will ever stomp into the office and demand a conference so they can tell the teacher this in front of the vice principal. It's our world. It like the media, finding some way they can put a miserable twist on everything. Reporting something positive doesn't sell, and my theory is that parents like the one above let their brains get scrubbed by all this. Whiney and irritable, we all know people like this. Their eyebrows are raised and crunched in, and nothing we say to them is going to help because they enjoy being miserable and they want to spread it around the school community like horseradish on sweet dark whole grain bread. God bless 'em. God bless 'em indeed.

In the end though, I have found parents to be valuable allies in the teacher's quest. But I gave up a long time ago dreaming that they will ever come out and be publicly and vocally supportive. It just isn't going to happen. It's that way with many of the silent majority factions. It would take something profoundly large to move them into this vocal frenzy. I think it's because they know vocal types to be very abrasive and they tend to make others bristle. Therefore they are not worth emulating. There's a higher chance of your dogs cleaning the toilets while you're away on vacation.

I See a Dinosaur But I Hear an Elephant

I am starting to get the idea that I am really different. I claim to be conservative. Conservatives seem to have gotten a bad rap though. Many people think that conservatives are either scripture barking haranguers or rich fat white guys out at the country club getting a massage. And there are a tremendous number of us who simply cannot be categorized there. Some of my teacher friends may claim that I simply cannot be categorized anywhere. And it is true, I suppose. I have this inner conflict inside of me about how teaching ought to be, as well as other social institutions.

I enjoyed my classical education. I have read Plato and Aristotle, and studied mathematics and logic (although the logic part is probably not readily evident). I play the piano. I have read the complete works of William Shakespeare, and have written music for four of his sonnets, thus far. I have performed in well over thirty plays and directed others. And I have written short plays as well. I very much enjoy history, if it's not written by radicals, and I am also fascinated by science, a D in college biology notwithstanding. I appear to have this balance on the outside, but the inner conflict still remains. As a teacher, I think there is a place for sit-down-at-your-desk discipline, and a time for out of your seat community service projects, or perhaps other creative endeavors.

For example, I have this idea that I really want to bring to fruition. I probably shouldn't mention it because one of you will run off and claim it as your own. What the hell, I'll tell you anyway. One night, I got this great idea for a musical that we could do in math class. It would be a one act, because I'm not sure I could write music for an entire two act version. Anyway, I envisioned the setting of a pirate ship (The H.M.S. Relation Ship) with the big opening number called "That Pythagorean Feeling". It would be basically a choral number with a few solo lines, and lots of dance breaks where the kids could tumble around stage with knives in their mouths.

And the plot, which most musicals refuse to use, would surround the finding of lost treasure that was eventually discovered using the famous Pythagorean Theorem. And the pirates get so excited about it that they calculate the mast height of their ship, so they could determine how far the captain would be dropped to the deck because he was found out to be a dirty two faced math teacher soliciting cheap child labor. The pirates then determine how long it will take the captain to fall this distance by using the formula for acceleration due to gravity, which they found tucked inside an out of tune piano in the galley.

Anyway, the plot would have to run swiftly because of the one act time length, and it could be sprinkled with other musical numbers such as "Hypotenuse Hype" and a big dance number called "C~Squared My Butt".

The problem is, I know that once I started in to it, some of the kids would simply not be able to handle it, and I would find myself wanting to sit them back down with me in the classroom doing my traditional teaching and sneezing on the overhead. I go back and forth with this. Nobody is sure if the kids are really learning anything in the musical anyway. I would have other math teachers standing around me shaking their heads in disgust and letting the air out of my car tires in the parking lot on their prep periods. I am always second guessing myself this way. I go back and forth. Sometimes I want to cut completely loose, but I fear that if I do, I will desperately want to return. Although some of you by now are wondering what being completely cut loose is if it isn't me now. I understand.

I share these with the kids by the way. I run my ideas past them and they get more excited than I do. But I can't tell if it's a good thing or if they have found another way to take advantage of me.

There's another idea I came up with in class. It just came to me one day when I was reviewing a homework assignment. It would be the story of a barrel shaped girl called *Cylinderella.* And she would have an obtuse step family of course, and all the other traditional pieces of the other story would remain, including her denial by the step mother to attend the prince's upcoming sphere. But again, I get too far with my ideas and I can see some of the kids inventing weapons when they should be backstage waiting for their cues, and the other math teachers would be off to the parking lot again sneaking around my car. I would find myself calling my toll free AAA number for help twice a month to get towed to a shop.

I have already used the balcony scene from *Romeo and Juliet* to teach the concept of slope. I did it entirely on the overhead though with popsicle puppets. The kids liked it, but again, the traditional side of me is constantly questioning the creative side. What attracted me to math in the first place was its quality of Truth, that it could be depended on because of its association with Beauty, or Quality. There was an essence to math that resonated very much with the romantic as well as the classical side of me. There is art and philosophy on every page. But how do I ever get kids to see what I see in it when I'm constantly making a mockery of it, and of myself? Maybe it's not a mockery but just a plain ineffective approach.

It's like I have to balance this traditional approach to it while taking risks with the other connections I see. And it turns out it has the same chemical make up as the battle that goes on inside of me. It's the same inner conflict that got me into trouble trading commodities on borrowed money. I knew it was unwise, but I did it anyway, perhaps thinking the romantic edge of my sword would carry me through.

Whenever I taught prime numbers I would always bring food coloring and jars of water in the class and spend half the period asking kids to show me what they know about blue, or what they know about purple. Using the "primary colors", they demonstrated what they were and how they could be used to make any color. They are very much the same thing as prime numbers, and this is very much the same as the Periodic Table of the Elements which we talk about as well. From there we moved on to the kids telling me what they know about 48 or 37, and we would make a natural progression to the Sieve of Eratosthenes and eventually prime and composite numbers.

I didn't necessarily think this was unwise, but as with most of what I do, I questioned myself and considered that I may have wasted my energy. I mean, why weren't primary colors mentioned or the Periodic Table mentioned in our book? Maybe that's why kids do so poorly in math, because people like me tend to stray.

I always get a kick out of teachers who say, "Ooh, whatever you do don't lecture them!" Anybody who says that simply doesn't know how to lecture. I've known many teachers, one in particular that was gifted at it. He always had the kids riveted to the topics because *he knew how to do it!* He was talented at it. Students that did nothing for me, produced for him. He was simply using his strength. All the in-service teachers say research shows that it's ineffective and doesn't lead to optimal learning. Horsefeathers! That's because all the people the researchers studied were truly boring and shouldn't have been lecturing in the first place! What is so hard about figuring that out?

So I battle these people, and I battle them every year. I can surely anticipate yet another in-service next year where our district will have paid way too much money for someone to come in and *lecture* us about how lecturing is ineffective and she will prove it to me by getting my butt numb for three and a half hours. She will prove it to me simply because she is horrible at it, and can't do it. Then to put *us* in the optimal state of learning in the afternoon, the district feeds us bologna sandwiches for lunch. I don't get it. Nothing is worse than being stuck in a room full of math teachers, made to stay through a working lunch when you're aching hungry with nothing but bologna sandwiches to eat. Its depressive condition is beyond description.

I always found it amusing that the latest and greatest ways to teach are often delivered to us in the methods that they are discouraging these days. It's a scream. Or, if it's a presenter that really tries to do it with the flare and the excitement that they think just readily activates and grips the kids, he is so awful at it that it gives me observer discomfort. It's like watching someone have a seizure. You want to step in and help but you know the best thing to do is to stay out of the way, let it run its course and make sure nobody gets hurt. (Maybe that psychology degree is coming in handier than I thought.) I don't mean to hinder the efforts of these people, but why don't they do what comes naturally? I believe they will reach many more people that way.

Teaching, and learning for that matter, is an art. It is not a science. There are some principles, I suppose, one should try to adhere to, but why not show teachers how to take advantage of their natural abilities and talents? Every one of these teacher trainers that come in acknowledges the *multiple* intelligences and the *many* different learning styles, but many of them can't see the foolishness of promoting one teaching style! This makes me so nuts that I fight the urge to stand up, scream, take off my shoes and pee in them!

If you ever get a chance, go find and read the poem "When I Heard the Learn'd Astronomer" by Walt Whitman. I about leaped out of my shoes when I read it late one night. I was working as a night watchman at the University of Idaho and it was about two o'clock in the morning. I carried this poetry book around with me one night and I stumbled on this poem. The speaker talks of being in a lecture given by an astronomer and how the professor was burying the audience in numbers and charts, and soon he grew unaccountably tired and burdened, I think. He can't find any escape or relief from his condition until he decides to stand up, walk out of the lecture and set himself in the presence of the perfectly sculpted glory of the stars in the night sky.

This is an *exact* emotion I have felt literally hundreds of times in my life. And this is an emotion that often starts swelling when I listen to the "learn'd teachers".

I haven't heard from any of the snoozer English teachers any complaints that Shakespeare didn't write enough expository pieces, or novels, or that he really didn't support his statements through research. They marvel at him for what he did do well, at least those English teachers did that can handle teaching a little Shakespeare.

Another thing that almost pushes me over the edge is that handout we teachers all get at one time or another. It says "We remember 10% of what we hear, 20% of what we hear and write, 30% of zzzz...." and so on all the way to something like "...90% of what we are active in!" And the first thing I think is this is concocted! Why does it increase in perfect ten-percent increments? Isn't that kind of a red flag that we teachers should catch on to immediately? Why doesn't anybody mention this?

Again, don't get me wrong. I am all for active learning. But what is *active* learning defined? What does it mean to be *active*? Do you have to be on two feet? Does the book have to be closed? When you are reading or listening does that mean your brain is *not* active? Don't they really mean active learning that is *more active* than simply active?

And so, my own conflict with this smolders. I am surrounded with people who look over their shoulders at the latest research, and then scream "Do it this way!! Do it this way!!" Then when the wind shifts, they shift as well, "No!! Do it the other way!!" It's like they are on a huge rudderless ship in a powerful wind screaming at us which way to steer, and they become frenzied because they don't know which direction the boat is headed either. Data based this, and data based that. My intuition tells me where to go as a teacher and for how long. Every artist or achiever I ever knew or read about, *even the ones we teach about in school* did this! Yet we, Public Education, think we have it right.

Abraham Lincoln failed at most everything, we all know that. He did his own thing. People were perfectly happy with the kerosene lamp before Edison came along. Did he ignore research? Or *was* he researching? Advisors to Fred Smith, founder of Federal Express said there was no market for his idea. Research showed it. The more I think about it, the more I want to take any research that's given to me in staff meetings and in-services, roll them up into giant cigarettes, smoke them in the boys room and tap the ashes into the sink in the staff room. My inner guide is telling me to reach for some balance, but that's not what all the "experts" are hollering for. It gets to be so agonizing listening to them.

I've only been teaching for ten years and I already sense that school teachers have outlived their usefulness. I've felt it for quite a few years now. Let me qualify this. The current trend in education is called "constructivism". Don't try looking it up because you won't find it outside of some scattered educational research circles. It involves self-discovery and building your own knowledge through your experiences. I have no problem with this. This is how I personally learned many things in my life. But when something becomes the be-all-and-the-end-all solution, that's where I start getting a little nervous. This is how cults start. Next thing you know they will be telling us all to take a taste of this new Kool-Aid someone came up with. It's like nobody ever heard of the middle of the boat. We all stampede to one side and then the other. Or like some new drivers. When they steer, they steer *all the way* to the right, and then *all the way* back to the left when they're done with the turn, only to steer all the way back to the right in order to correct themselves again for going all the way to the left. Back and forth this goes. Next thing you know, my stomach is getting ready to evict its tenants. What is wrong with letting the tires straighten out for awhile *until* it is necessary to turn again?

So with this new system called constructivism, the teacher becomes a "teacher", and the Gods of Education want to refer to you as "facilitator". We are to be this being that floats around on the side of all the activity, to handle logistics, the scheduling, the details, and to redirect kids' questions back to them. We become some type of project manager. Once again, I honestly believe there is a time for this! I am certainly not throwing it out entirely. But when it becomes the latest dominant and pervasive technique, I feel like I've become part of this grasping-at-straws-knee-jerk-reaction crowd mentality. It's like telling a carpenter he can only use a saw from now on. Nothing else. What? You use a nail gun? How not-with-it you simply have become! You are stuck in the past and refuse to grow; you must be a...*conservative!!!*

Anyway, back to my qualifying argument about having outlived my usefulness as a school teacher. If I'm to be this unimportant, secondary if not tertiary figure, *why am I needed at all?* Why don't they hire class secretaries, reduce the salaries and get rid of "teachers". Can't we be *progressive* and eliminate the need for such archaic, and conservative figureheads? Actually, there are online schools popping up all over the country. Kids are taking entire courses via the internet without having to look into the eyes of anyone. Home school networks are tapping in to this diddy. (By the way I support the efforts of the home school movements. As soon as the NEA finds this out, they're going to send over

Moose and Rocko…again.) Why don't I just roll out the cardboard cut out of Mr. Powell, push it out into the front of the class and let him rip? The only way I've discovered that keeps kids' attention on me anyhow is wearing a television monitor over my head. They immediately bow down to the one-eyed god.

MTV and movies and video games and computers are educating the kids anyway! Where is my importance? Where is the significance of what I offer? And don't tell me they really need me because of the sneezing on the overhead trick, it isn't going to fly. And don't tell me that they need the human interaction and real people looking into their eyes, not that I don't believe in that need. It's just that another trend is to step out of their way and let technology in and do its thing. What I can't swallow though is the teacher trainers who promote this new method, yet still appear to cling to the notion that kids need to be taught by humans!

So between technology and constructivism who needs school teachers? If the people business of teaching really needed the people part of it, there would be an emphasis on it. And I do not see the emphasis. We say they are needed but we show otherwise. It's like those old movies from the fifties about dinosaurs. You see the dinosaur, but they always overdubbed the sound of a trumpeting elephant. So it is with teaching…I see a dinosaur, but I hear an elephant.

Of course I know why teachers are needed. Maybe now more than ever it's time to put the eyes of the little ones in front of the classroom more of the time. Do we really expect them to teach themselves for the majority of the day? Where has common sense gone? Where's the balance?

So I resort to strategies that do nothing but stir the conflict inside of me. Strategies like musicals on a pirate ship. Me and my wonderful ideas. I wrote a little skit one time about the distributive property. (Skits? In math class? Yes! I told a group of parents one time on "Back to School Night" that I was "skits-oh-phrenic" because I did them once in awhile in class. Some of them didn't get it. I had to explain to my principal the next day why some parents had some concerns with me sharing my personal problems, and then *I* didn't get it.)

Anyway, I noticed that kids weren't following through completely with the distributive property when I taught it the traditional way so I wrote a very short play called *The Short But Important Story of Demetrius the Kind Boy.* And the kids got it. Whenever they saw an expression that needed the distributive property to simplify, they identified the important pieces by character names from my skit, and this was months after they learned it.

The problem with it was that I had high school teachers catch up to me a few years later and say, "Okay Powell, who the hell is Demetrius?" They weren't happy about having to undo the "mess" I created with my plays. I thought who cares what they call the integers and variables as long as they are doing it properly! Where's the harm in that? Leave it to a math teacher to *not* get this.

But I do agree with them to a point. I also agree mathematics needs to remain pure in many cases. It's like fresh vegetables versus frozen vegetables enhanced with a little too much sodium. We all know what's more nutritious; it's just that sometimes I want to make it easier for it to slide down.

Many years ago I had to teach seventh graders about the Arab-Israeli conflict and I wrote a play called *The Oily Hand or the Pail of Stone?* (The Holy Land or Palestine) in which the main characters revealed themselves and their motives: *Julie, Judy, and Julian* (the Jewish), the *Romancers*

(Roman Empire), *Eric, Aaron, and Errol* (Arabs), *Got Bitten (a bulldog)* (Great Britain) and others. I also introduced some places too; *The Worst Bag* (The West Bank) and *Guys Are Drips* (Gaza Strip) and so on. It's fun for the kids to participate in these, and they do get the basic framework of the conflict, but how is this going to help them on a standardized test? I don't know. Does it matter? Yes! Well, no. Maybe it does.

And this is how the self-tormenting of Mr. Powell continues year after year. I just don't get some things. In one of my earlier years of teaching, there was a teacher in our district who the principal claimed was an exemplary model of teaching excellence. This teacher *highly* praised and rewarded students for spitting out all the capitals from the South American continent in less than 12 seconds. He took them to McDonald's for lunch. My first reaction was that it was stupid and useless, not to mention personally costly, but the principal assured me that it was because I was a new teacher and didn't understand it all yet. That was ten years ago and I think less of it now than I did then. I haven't learned a thing.

Perhaps I shouldn't be a teacher. I know some parents who would cheer for an occasion such as my decision to leave teaching, just as some of the radical liberals kept chilled champagne ready to celebrate the death of Ronald Reagan. (*That* was creepy, to think people actually did this.) I feel like Herbie from *Rudolph the Red-Nosed Rain Deer*, a misfit, except he was pretty much committed to his dentist thing.

Yikes. I don't even know where to go from here. I may be the only math teacher in the country who teaches the math in *Hamlet*, but I'm certain I'm not the only one who gets irritated with those signs in the staff rooms, *If you're*

not interested in change, you're not interested in growth.
Or this one, *Change is inevitable.* Neither one of these
is completely true by the way. I like change just as much
as the people who are giddy changeophiles, it's just that I
especially like it under the pretense of a damn good reason,
and not whims. Everything does not change anyway,
here's proof: Living here on earth, we do not change our
accountability for gravity. If I jump out of an airplane, I
will *always expect to fall.* This perspective will not change.
Additionally, there is one other thing that will never change;
the *Truth* will never change.

Wrap your arms around those for awhile. I did, and I
made the mistake of telling some other teachers about it and
they spent an agonizing ten minutes trying to pry my arms
loose. The fact that these people didn't even pause to "let it
resonate", like bells after they stop ringing, was a terrifying
sign to me. Are we teachers really like that?

I don't know how long I can last. Maybe I should've
been a monk. Some people think I'm already half way there
because in my house we have no television and we haven't
had for about sixteen years. That's right, no TV. We have
a television monitor but no channels, no cable, no antennae,
no satellite, nothing. We watch VHS tapes and DVDs. It is
absolute heaven. I had a student one time that sassed back
at me, "How can you live in a cave like that?" I told him
it's my job to work in a cave with a bunch of pre-historic
primates, I am used to it.

Many kids and a few adults fear that I become
disconnected with the world around me by living this way,
but they have no idea what I remain connected *to* that
counts. Many things in our culture are worth disconnecting
from anyway, pop culture idiots for example. I was standing
in line at the grocery store one time and on the cover of

one of those dopey magazines, they announced the list of the fifty most important pop culture icons. You can tell immediately that these magazines are written by idiots for idiots. Michael Jackson? Wacko Jacko? An *important* pop culture icon? This guy's freak show makes me look like Mr. Rogers. Michael Jackson is completely *gone*.

Most of you won't relate to this, but when you spend so much time away from television, and you happen to walk by a Sears TV display and see an excerpt from some sitcom, it strikes you as the most imbecilic creation for even a reptilian brain. Is this what our society thinks is worthwhile now? And these "reality" TV programs are refuse beyond the landfill of the mind. They are about as real as professional wrestling. They follow the same formula! They change the way they are acting because they are being watched! How the hell hard is that to figure out?

I know what you're thinking. I can sense you trying to connect the dots. Maybe this is why Mr. Powell is so "out there". If he would only reconnect with the world around him and attune his mind to the things that kids these days find important, he will fall in love with teaching and gain his sanity back. No thanks. My insanity is derived from being one of six teachers in the nation who can actually see this pop culture at work doing what it was designed to do, namely, drum critical thinking out of the realm of normalcy and wildly celebrate stupidity of very high degrees.

I know there is positive programming. My own children are not suffering. They see "channels" as they call them at Grandma's house or over at Aunt Laura's, but I will do all I can to keep my children my responsibility and not the property of the idiots of mass media.

We see a tremendous amount of good programming through rentals from the public library and commercial stores. But they spend time reading, being read to, and experiencing plenty of eyeball to eyeball interaction with all of their family. We are as close as a modern day *Walton's* family. We have even been known to do puppet shows behind the Lazy Boy, or even impromptu plays on the living room floor before bed time. I want my kids to have at least some of their imagination intact before the rest of the world tries to trivialize and disqualify it. I wish my students at school were more of the same.

Maybe this is what pushes me closer to the edge in the classroom. I know that I'm never going to win this battle, I know that I'm only one man and ultimately not necessary and I find that frustrating. I heave a huge sigh of despair every time I see a normally wild kid settle right down when he's drugged up with the TV or when a computer or video game is shoved in front of his face, bringing him down as if he just received something intravenously. Kids are all born these days with computer skills, but many lack the simple ability to interact successfully with people. And what may bother me most is that I seem to be the only one worried about this.

Where the Earth Meets the Sky

There was this toilet seat in the men's bathroom in a middle school where I used to work, that was the most ergonomically designed seat in the district. I can say this with some authority because I've been around. A man could close the door, sit down, close his eyes and see where he fits into the grand design from there. The clocks stopped. And when he returned from whence he came, not one second had ticked by. This is just what the character Elwood P. Dowd said in the play *Harvey,* about what his invisible rabbit friend could do. Not sit on a toilet seat, but stop a clock and take a guy somewhere else.

And the ironic twist about this is that a guy didn't want to be any place else. It wasn't that the men's bathroom was such a great place to be, but this particular school was.

I remember reading a story one time about a man who rode his bicycle across America backward. He sat on the handle bars and pedaled slowly in reverse. Of course he had brakes and he was wont to use them in appropriate or ideal conditions. His premise was that he preferred to see where he had been rather than contend with the present. He could well reflect more clearly and accurately, and spend more time piecing everything together this way. I suppose he would have to look forward every now and then, and I don't remember if he had a team to help him achieve this or not, but I do remember it made no sense to me at the time.

It was one of those ten speed bicycles popular in the seventies with the handle bars that looked like the antlers of a bighorn sheep. And I imagine he had it modified to suit his purposes. It's hard to believe a man who lived like this would not have been required to make many modifications.

Of course, as I have found out all through my life, even the smallest events that I had no ability to grasp at the time have returned many years later to complete some "cycle" and fulfill its purpose. If you've ever read any T.S. Eliot poems, you may know what I mean. The man floods the reader with such a tremendous number of images, that one has no hope of grasping them all. Yet when you're done, or when a great deal of time has passed, you're left with something still. Maybe it's like panning for gold. You're not always going to have a nugget when you're done, but you're sure to have none if you don't look. It's more common in my life anyway to be left with flakes not nuggets. But you know, the flakes add up.

There was this computer science class I took in college years ago. I think it was Pascal. I earned a C in the class. I was no Jimmy Neutron. But the language of it intrigued me and the course passed so quickly that I couldn't let go of my fascinations soon enough to be ready to grasp what was coming next. It was very engaging for me, but I was not a particularly good *student* in the class. The note taking, the organizational challenges, and meeting assignment deadlines were difficult for me. Or perhaps I chose to make them an issue. I would've been horrible on a circus trapeze.

People would come pay money to watch me swing back and forth until I was damn good and ready to move on. A stampede to get their money back would soon follow.

Nonetheless, three or four weeks after the course ended, I was still fiddling around with some of the programs I wrote. It struck me one night in a computer lab, that I knew enough about programming to go back and be an A student. In the time limit of the course, I only had the capacity in me to be average. But not one month later, long after the grades had been turned in, I was far better. After the class was done, and after I had a chance to let it percolate and stew, I was able to make some sense out of it.

And this brings me back to this man who rode his bicycle backward. Suddenly, this image of him returns and it is meaningful to me. I understand him. But I don't think I understand him enough to articulate it to someone else. This is a common theme that has been weaving through my life like a drunk on a sidewalk. This idea of things previously misunderstood or mishandled by me often come back and crystallize, like ice out of thin cold air, into something that is sensible, yet intangible and still distant.

Try telling what I just told you to a high school math teacher. I can just see one in particular staring at me right now. She's grinding her back teeth as she listens, and is nervously bouncing one foot back and forth and up and down. She's glaring at me like I'm the driver of a late bus she's waiting for. My presence has forced her to the border of her comfort zone, and she is probably irritated because she was trying to balance her checkbook in her head and I have ruptured her concentration with silly philosophizing. *Get rid of the tool belt Powell. You're mishandling the education of kids.* This did not really happen, but I was captured by the idea that it could have happened if I slipped. I have slipped in the past, by the way.

The man on the bicycle knows this. He is aware of the forces that facilitate his journey. And my recycled thoughts somehow are coming back to patch things up, like a mason scooping away extra mortar on a wall or foundation that needed mending.

These are probably not the thoughts you'd expect to hear from a middle school math teacher. It's amazing where sitting on a toilet seat can take you. I'm not sure these are thoughts of an active brain searching for meaning or a lost brain looking for a way out. I cannot deny it: I am a seeker.

Many years ago, like many people do, I struggled with the idea of God and the Infinite. I had read a lot of Ralph Waldo Emerson and one phrase, among many, has imbedded itself on my psyche. It came from his essay *Self-Reliance*. He writes, "We lie in the lap of immense intelligence, which makes us receivers of its truth and organs of its activity." He also wrote an essay titled *Circles* where he says "the eye is the first circle and the horizon which it forms is the second". He also writes, "Our life is an apprenticeship to the truth that around every circle another can be drawn; that there is no end in nature, but every end is a beginning; that there is always another dawn risen on mid-noon, and under every deep a lower deep opens." (I actually extended an extra credit assignment to some geometry students one time to read this essay and write a reflection paper. I had one taker and, incidentally, it was the kid who lobbed up his lunch on my classroom floor, though it was a couple of years later that he tackled this challenge.)

So with respect to Emerson, sometimes I feel like I don't even get a circle drawn, before another one begins.

I mismanage time and somehow let it pass through my hands without giving the events therein the proper attention. There are no endings he seems to say, only beginnings. New dawns and opportunities to begin again abound.

It seems that my life has been like a fast moving glacier that tills up things in its path, but I lack a stronger, more dominating ability to make some order out of them. So I remedy this by thinking out loud and by writing, after the fact of course. Where does the math fit into this all? Mathematics has been a life preserver to me in confusing times because of its perfection. It is the mortar. It helps me attach myself to a foundation. It keeps me grounded.

Then somehow this gave birth to thoughts and constructs of mine that extended for months. Eventually, I decided that there was a Creator, God. In addition though, there were other beings. I could feel them there with Him. I could see where they were when I walked to my college classes. Perhaps it was self-centered of me, but I felt as if they were assigned to me. To watch and guide. They made me a better person, and a more disciplined student. They knew my faults, and they were aware of all of my failures. They remained highly aware of my eccentricities, but they continued to encourage that side of me that was made to help others. It was almost as if I had known them before too, and I could always find them where the earth meets the sky.

Years later, deep into my teaching career, I narrowly escaped a high school teaching assignment by just a few days. I thought I wanted a new job teaching high school math. Our district was building two new replacement high schools and reconfiguring grade levels in buildings. I had actually interviewed for and was granted a position at one of these schools. However, there was a year and a half wait until it began due to building construction and so forth.

I had been at this school for several years. But previous to the new high school positions opening up we had new administrator come in to replace a retiree. She was a very good principal but only stayed one year. We all thought she was in it for the long haul, but an assistant superintendent position from a neighboring district, her former employer, came open. I remember the day she told the staff she was leaving. My first thought was that this must be similar to what kids go through when their parents divorce. It's probably a good thing that she left because I never would've even considered leaving if she was still there. Her desire to move on and "draw new circles" inspired me to do the same.

So, within that year and a half before moving to the high school, things began to emerge. Among them was my decision that I really wanted to be with vivacious and cheery middle school kids versus the morose wearers of morbid make-up for the living. Some of these high school kids today are exceedingly pathetic. They drag themselves around like walking corpses wearing nothing but black clothing, black lipstick, chains and spiked accessories. Their feet don't even leave the ground; the kids shuffle like the handicapped back and forth to their smoking areas with their pants down around their knees. And then they are paranoid about being stared at! I could never figure them out! They want so badly to be "different" and to draw some type of value out of their subculture attire, and to express themselves to the world with pierced heads only to be offended when someone looks at them, *when it's what they all want in the first place!*

Anyway, it turned out also to be an issue of wanting to work with a different middle school administration. I needed to experience middle school from a new perspective. As things evolved, it looked like I wouldn't be able to get a reversal on my decision to return to the middle level. Only the summer months remained and there was no activity on an opening. There had to be an opening in order for me to return.

But I kept my faith over those months that *something* would make itself available, and just a few short days before school started, Horizon Middle School found me. I walked into the interview knowing no one and left feeling like I could work there forever, and I hadn't even been offered the job yet.

One of the first people I met was Rosanna the secretary. She and her partner in office management, Deanne, as in many organizations set the tone for the school atmosphere. World class is a term normally associated with athletes or musicians. But I refuse to describe these two with anything else but the words world class. They had nothing but talent and an unbelievable way of making the middle school a simple, streamlined process.

They were people who had uncanny intuitive skills to maintain the flow of administrative data and keep it circulating in its proper direction, if you know what I mean. And when they ever got off the phone with parents who were getting too big for their britches, they would know exactly how to capture the essence of the matter and express it with language one could really put their arms around.

The day I moved in and received my room assignment, Dan the head custodian's help was all over me like leather on a cow. One after the other, the staff in this school made it known that their workplace was about each other. And even though I was happy with the staff at my other school, I knew I was in for something special here. In fact, I felt somewhat guilty that I began to enjoy them more in a collective sense.

And this brings me again back to the man who rode backward, the lap of immense intelligence, and circles. And it also brought me back to the other Godly presence of people that I couldn't see, but I knew were there. The school that I let get away was where the earth meets the sky. It has been a long story and over a year since I left them, for reasons I still haven't turned completely around to understand yet. And for all the talk I put forth about appeasing administrators and overly giddy teachers, I do not characterize Horizon Middle School this way.

Middle school teachers are generally the best to be around. They don't tend to be overly uptight like high school teachers and definitely are not as overwhelming as elementary school types. Elementary school teachers tend to bury me with curriculum teacher talk, and boy can they talk, talk, talk, talk, talk, and talk. No wonder high school teachers get annoyed. God bless them, just keep them away. Being around them is like trying to swim through a pool of barley syrup; they are simply exhausting. Their vision isn't big enough. They see school kids, while I see kids. My wife frowns at me for this because she is an elementary school teacher, but she's a music specialist which makes her different. She is also a middle school teacher as well and a thousand times more balanced than any female elementary teacher I ever met. Julie is a full time worker, but a part time teacher. She knows how to attend to her sensibilities, talents and balance. In my opinion, this is not the norm.

High school teachers tend to sit at meetings and look at their watches. Arms are usually crossed in a somewhat defiant posture, and what they have to say they say in the bluntest way available. Not that I am not blunt. But it goes beyond this for many of these types. They don't like talkers. Especially competitive endurance talkers like elementary teachers. Some of them even find themselves way too caught up in classroom dogma. In this way, they are similar to elementary teachers, but don't tell *them* that. Often they are fiddling with the change in their pockets, and they tend to scowl at meeting leaders for even the thought of having one. Oh yeah, and they grind their teeth a lot too. But give them a break, all levels of teaching drive people to irrational, rough or other irritating behaviors.

Middle school teachers simply have the worst meeting behavior of them all. (You thought I was going to jump off right there and start praising them didn't you? Not a chance!) We are the clear and present winners of the teachers-behaving-badly category. But, partially because of this, they are more fun to be around. It's difficult to get a bunch of us to shut up at a meeting because we rejoice in the presence of each other. It's finally a time to tell each other who accidentally farted in class, or who chucked up in the hall, and what it looked like and all that fun stuff that elementary teachers frown at us for bringing up because it's "unprofessional". High school teachers frown at us for it too because, you know, *somebody's got to be an adult around here.* Which brings me again to where the earth meets the sky.

At Horizon Middle School, there wasn't a more diverse group of teachers. (I hate using that word *diverse* around teachers because their interpretation of it becomes tremendously artificial. That's all I can say about it, except if you want to know more about what I think of it, I refer you to *Diversity: the Invention of a Concept* by Peter Wood.)

To begin with there was our vice principal, Denis. I don't know how he ended up in education, but the man is genuinely talented, and funny. I mean this in a positive way. He has so much enthusiasm for his staff. This is a guy who starts talking about the Christmas party in September. This is a party *for* the staff given *by* the staff.

This is the only school I ever worked in where it was mostly the men that did all the skits and the performing. And it included Dan the custodian. At my other schools it always seemed to be me, maybe one other guy, and the rest women. Anyway, this particular year I wrote a Christmas skit for us all called *The Jolly Fat Bastard*. It revolved around Santa's bad mood one year. A few elves notice and thought they could help the situation, cheer up Santa (played by Denis) and save Christmas by slipping some cooking sherry into Mrs. Claus's evening hot chocolate (Mrs. Claus played by our *principal* Laurie, the former high school drama teacher). This would then make Mrs. Claus cheery and "seasonally festive", and therefore seep over into JFB's attitude and persuade him to be more festive as well. The plot was also thickened with Viagra (Denis's idea). No pun intended of course.

So we did this little show and sang some of those Christmas songs where the lyrics have been irreverently changed. We actually *rehearsed*. It was not one of those gigs where you show up and just wing it. Those are simply agonizing to do and to watch. I've done plenty of those before but this was strictly professional and down to business, and consequently it was fun and entertaining.

At this school, it was not uncommon for me to slip across the hall and sing a song or two with Sonny the science teacher. We actually did two small gigs that year. One was singing one of my Shakespeare sonnet songs to the office staff on Shakespeare's birthday, and the other was doing "Home on the Range" at a westward movement culmination project. Sonny played the guitar and I played my little keyboard.

We could sit in the lunch room and talk about the conservative teachers in the world, both of them, about how stale and flat they are, and then refer to all the liberal teachers and tease them about how the great amounts of pot they smoked being the reason that they simply can't quite get it.

The kids were also different. This was in a neighborhood that definitely drew a different type of kid generally from a more traditional family. The families seemed to place more of an emphasis on academics at this school I noticed. I could also tell the kids were different than anywhere I had been because when I was standing in the hall and whipped out Bucky, my own hand made sock puppet from my tool belt, and had him start in to a Richard III monologue, the kids didn't walk by and grab him and twist his eyeballs off. (This actually happened in another school. This is what TV and video games do to some kids. It kills their compassion and renders them ill-equipped to interact with live "street theatre". Coarse and unrefined hallway brutality.)

Well, long after I hot-glued Bucky's face back together, I got the courage to try him out in the hall at Horizon and he was well received. I could tell he was because the kids walked by and looked sideways at Bucky and I, pretending not to notice while they bee lined for their next classroom. They warmed up to it though.

I made puppets out of everything. Bucky, like I said, was constructed from a wool sock. I have made other puppets out of glue containers, tennis balls, and staplers.

One of my favorites is Ray the One-Eyed-Eraser, which not surprisingly I made out of a dry eraser-board eraser. He is simply beyond description, and I don't find it necessary to describe him anyway, other than he also lives in my tool belt tucked in the back pocket where a carpenter might keep a tape measure, and he has a tongue and a bit of red fluffy hair. The point is all of these characters seemed to be well received at this school. *Not* that riots broke out at other schools when impromptu puppet performances began. I have to tell you though, when Bucky was mauled I was soured. (Math teachers across America are inexplicably getting gas right now. *Puppets?*) I wanted to boot the kid's butt six ways from Sunday. His mom claimed, "You shouldn't have had it out in the hall if you didn't want it ruined by kids!" (Yeah, right lady. How about grabbing a brain and joining the human race with the rest of us. You can tell who's in charge in her home.)

School years can be characterized by several ups and downs, periods of high stress, mild to moderate vomiting, high fevers, hives and the shakes. Probably like other careers out there. Perhaps Janet Jackson's career for example. As she lobbed her boob out into American homes during the Stupor Bowl, I'm sure her life of whirlwind stress intensified, being her position is important to our youth. The one year I spent at Horizon though, was without question the most even tempered, stress-less, efficient and pleasant school year I have ever recorded. I remember sitting by my desk about a week and a half into the job thinking to myself that I could stay here forever. Denis walked into my room at about that time to see how things were going. He had that type of stride where his hands were stuffed in his pockets and his legs and feet slowly and stiffly swung wide. I told him I had never been as pleased.

It all begins with leadership. Laurie and Denis were there for the right reasons. They were people persons, and they led by example. I personally saw Laurie extinguish several situations at our school that were daily occurrences at another school I taught at. Consequently, the behaviors were rarely seen again. Kids are kids and they are going to try to find out where and how thick the dark line is between what they can get away with and what they can't. And it doesn't matter what socioeconomic level the kids come from, they are all there to look for this line. Laurie showed them exactly where the line was, and exactly how thick it was going to be as long as she was in charge. This was funny to watch the kids' faces when they realized they found the line and its subsequent thickness. I loved it. They looked like they just ran into a wall, eyeballs circling around and all. She never had her head stuck up in the clouds, I never felt as if she sat in an ivory tower, she was always very personable, and she had this uncanny ability to influence me to work extra hard for her goals, if for no other reason than her willingness to support the teachers. She also knew how to shield her staff from the trivial tripe that often swirls around schools, generated by parents or other administrators outside the building. If she didn't think it was going to help by passing along useless, picky or offensive information, by golly it ended with her right there. God bless Laurie.

I have never seen a school assembly that ended unexpectedly twenty minutes early, when teachers or the administration didn't panic and try to pass it with hand wringing and looking the other way. Never. That is until I saw Denis, Laurie's assistant, skillfully bring these situations to a close. This means nothing to a person who's never been in this situation. When you have an assembly with the entire middle school student body, a lot of planning and preparation precedes it. This includes teachers *not* planning for their class times because it is occupied by the activities at the assembly. And when it ends without warning twenty minutes before school is out, you have a slight problem on your hands. Remember, kids are like chlorine gas, they are more toxic the more concentrated they are. And when you have them all concentrated in the bleachers with nothing in front of them, it will be like *Lord of the Flies* faster than free beer disappears at a hockey game.

Denis, hops up from his chair, grabs the microphone and speaks to the student body. A kid could be sitting there in a crowd of five hundred and feel like Denis was talking personally to him. He begins a game that involves the entire school by pulling several representatives from each grade level down to the floor to participate. He narrates the action, again to the spectators, the kids are cheering and the next thing you know they *have* to stop because the after school buses are waiting and ready to go.

Of course it doesn't end there. As assistant principal he has to be all over the kids with discipline issues, and he can be a hammer. But he also spends a couple days a week after school playing card games of some sort with a small group of kids. This he does on his own time. I never did figure out what game it was that he was playing with them though. (Maybe *that's* how he built up such a collection of CD players and cigarette lighters in his office!)

He used to be a counselor which is a fantastic background if you want to move into this position, but you can't bring the wimpy counselor with you. You must do it with the firm counselor. God bless Denis.

I have never had a finer pair of people to work for in my teaching career, nor was a team of teachers to work with more close and supportive. A combination like this will never happen again. It may be commonplace in other career areas, but in my experience it is rare in education. It is like Halley's Comet, I'll see it again in seventy six years. Maybe.

I am on the bicycle looking backward at these wonderful people. I have attempted to draw another circle around them, and so far it hasn't worked. I haven't wanted it to either. I am appealing to the immense intelligence from its lap. The day I left them I presented Mr. Powell's top twelve list of things I would miss about HMS. Here they are word for word:

12. The shock I experienced after imitating Patrick from *Sponge Bob Square Pants*, after which a student bluntly told me, "You don't get along with adults very well, do you Mr. Powell?"
11. Mrs. Smallfoot's gentility when I went in and told her that I was looking for my wedgie.
10. The district's most ergonomically designed toilet seat in the men's bathroom.
9. My very own 504 plan...that allows me to do the slobbering, prehistoric bit whenever I damn well please.
8. The casual, but cavalier way that Mrs. Stranberg announced to the second lunch staff that a "shit load" of eighth graders weren't going on the Silverwood (amusement park) trip.
7. The looks on parents faces as I whistled "If I Only Had a Brain" on Back to School Night.
6. Christmas, thongs, and being able to call Denis a "Jolly Fat Bastard".

5. The laughter from Mrs. Cunningham's 3rd period class when she told them my ass was too big for my tool belt. (I found out later she actually said "abs".)

4. Mr. Smith's t-shirts…you know, the ones that he spray paints on. (muscular guy, tighter than average shirts)

3. The kindness of Mrs. Tibbits to let me slip back into my hillbilly vernacular, and pretend that I'm a younger, retarded brother.

2. The tolerance of my pod-mates Shelley, Margie and Mike (and sometimes Ann and Sharon) to really understand that I just HAD to try out the sneezing snot/ Windex trick on the pod windows.

1. The look of denial on Mrs. Moffit's face when she caught me, alone, making chimpanzee noises by my classroom door.

So here I am, sitting on my bicycle looking backward at Horizon Middle School. An opportunity came up to apply for and work in a school for a different kind of learner. I thought that it was what I wanted and where a teacher with my wacky disposition needed to be and grow. I was accepted, and I left Horizon after only one year.

It was a very difficult decision for me and I remember thinking at the time that it could turn out to be a disaster, but it was all part of the journey. It has been a year since I've been away and people asked me, "Did you have a good school year?"

"No." I replied, "But I learned a lot."

Where the earth meets the sky is not always in front of you. It could be in any direction you look. You just need to know which direction it is you want to go. Unfortunately, this has not always been easy for me to establish. Horizon was an ideal school that was steeped in something deep that was good for me to grow in. Emerson claims that "under every deep, a lower deep opens." But I'm not sure I was ready or willing to go deeper. And now that I know where I've been, I'm not absolutely sure that I *don't* want to turn around and go back for a second, longer look.

Thoroughly Neural

Every time I hear the word *progressive* escape someone's lips, it's possible that I could get slightly agitated. People can get very stingy with words. Whoever stampedes to it first and lays claim to it is the only one who can use it, it sometimes seems. And if it is ever used after this point, then it is by loan or permission only of those who claimed it from the beginning. Like Donald Trump and his dopey use of the phrase, "You're Fired" from his inane television program. He wants it as a registered trademark or something. I suppose it is similar with land, too. Generally, property is owned by one who is being productive with it in some capacity. Even so, ownership at times gets obnoxious. For example, trying to own a view of nature, say of Mt. Rainer is utterly ludicrous. And so it is similar with the word *progressive*. To me, it is a code word, meaning a liberal.

Well since the liberals claimed at least one derivation of this word as their own, and since they are being very "productive" with it, it makes perfect sense that they should be entitled to use it as a code word. I have no problem with that. I think that politically, at least in the United States anyway, it came in as part of a presidential campaign of the Progressive Party during the election years of 1912, 1924, and 1948. (I know, this is something that a middle school math teacher should *not* know.)

But being *progressive* to me does not necessarily mean being progressive, if you know what I mean. If I'm around a group of teachers that I don't know, I always try to avoid the word altogether. It's just too risky that they'll peg me for somebody I most certainly am not. Next thing you know, they start inviting me to a drag queen show, a protest march, diversity or sensitivity training seminars, or a We-need-to-get-rid-of-white-male-teachers candle party. Other than that, I enjoy using the word progressive to mean "developing to a more advanced level", or "advancing in stages". I especially like the latter.

I think it was smart for the liberals to grab it when they did because now they can try to show that if you're not liberal, or progressive, than you must be someone who wants to drive civilization back to the Dark Ages, to bring back the plague and so forth, hence a conservative. But everybody wants "advancement" (Except maybe the radical subhuman Islamo-Nazis that enjoy flying jumbo jets into skyscrapers) but from what reference point and in what direction? We're back to the concentric circles formed by a pebble thrown in a pond that Emerson wrote of.

I have been weight training in a gym for almost twenty three years. (Stay with me, this is relevant.) I remember a friend of my brother's told me I was never going to be big and strong. He was one of those smart asses in school, and maybe the reason that I began training in the first place. When I started, I was eighteen years old and maybe 175 pounds. This was at least four years after I was told to give it up by our friend the thirteen year-old expert. I was long and thin, an ectomorph in gym language. I am not naturally strong and I have medium bone size. It took me years to reach a body weight of 200 pounds, close to eight years. This is probably because I was overtraining using techniques that were improper for a guy at my level, because most people make better progress than that. I really had very little idea what I was doing. Nonetheless, I kept at it without the advice of a coach, just the overpriced magazines that were really written to sell their silly products. But I didn't figure this out for many years.

After several months of training and really not knowing what I was doing, I could bench press 205 pounds once. This is not an amazing feat. Many people with little or no training could do this. Twenty three years later I am at a body weight of a solid 228 pounds and I warm up my bench press workout with 225 pounds, and I can bench press 330 pounds once. And it is similar with other movements I do in the gym, not just bench pressing.

My point is I used *progressive* weight resistance techniques for years. This is a useful technique that I had learned to use from the beginning, although I experimented with different variations of it. I began with a weight that I could handle and as time passed, I used a little more weight and I didn't progress until I learned how to master it. I made absolutely sure that I was thoroughly neurally ready to move on so I wouldn't get injured and delay my progress. There's nothing wrong with challenging yourself from time to time, but they need to be tactical challenges. And perhaps I was over-cautious at times but good things take time. All good things take time.

I believe in the crockpot not the microwave. If you put a frozen burrito in the microwave you run the risk of it coming out cold in the middle because you're trying to prepare it too quickly. I tried to tell this to a group of parents-on-afterburners one night. They all wanted to know when their sons and daughters were going to be into trigonometry and calculus. I tried to tell them that education is not an avalanche that you want to bury kids under, especially math education. It tends to makes them cranky and starts up old bed wetting habits again, and other conditions like it. At least it did with me when I was a kid. They can't breathe and consequently die when they're smothered. By the way, they were seventh graders. Some of these kids in question didn't even know what a radius was.

And of course I would relate my weight training analogy to them and it went over like corned beef and sauerkraut. Telling them that their kids were not ready was something they did not want to accept. I insulted them. But today results need to be seen in microseconds not months or years, or it is archaic. What can I say, I know better. A lot of good people know better. But when push comes to shove these types of people simply say that I am most certainly not *progressive* enough for their tastes. I am not new, not hip, not with it, not up on pop culture, not "willing to change", or I'm "afraid to change". Imagine that. Me, the only psychopathic math teaching nut case in the country who is willing to portray Shakespeare's *Titus Andronicus* in class (in a less bloody, more symbolic way) and somehow make it relate, and *I'm* the one who is not *progressive* enough! *I'm* the one who resists change!

Progressive to me is advancing in stages, and at an appropriate pace, especially with mathematics. But I will also refer to it as "developing to a more advanced level", as in improving something, like educational techniques. And now you're thinking, Powell is a closet liberal because he wants to improve something. No, I am most certainly not a closet liberal, and yes I do want to improve something. And after all the self-disclosing I've done so far, you would think I would be telling the truth.

The difference between me and liberal teachers is this: They want a new ideology in the curriculum. They are rabid for multi-culturalism, and sensitivity training and *diversity* training, and worried that the school is "too white" (*Too white?* A counselor actually said this at a school once. Could this possibly be due to *indigenous demographics and NOT racism???*). They believe we should tolerate everybody, and by God I mean everybody including the violent, stupid and felonious (But of course we white males are right out). They want Christmas abolished, but Ramadan and this American invention called Kwanza can still exist. They don't want "Merry Christmas" on the tongues or minds of anyone in school, but they are okay with "Happy Rama-Hannu-Kwanz-Mas". All cultures, religions and languages are welcome with open arms as long as American, Christian, and English are not uttered among them or even thought of.

I as a conservative on the other hand want the traditional ideals of rigorous and worthwhile disciplines and I want extreme thinking to be a focus, except I want it *taught progressively.* I want more of the classical education re-introduced but I want the *way* we teach to be profoundly teacher, kid and brain friendly. If a teacher is a talented and gifted lecturer, I want him in my school badly. Someday, this will be considered a *progressive* teaching technique, if teaching by people survives that is. People will yearn to sit down and look into the eyes of an expert, and listen to them talk dynamically about worthwhile, life-changing events. It's called the *oral tradition,* you know, that thing that the liberals shoved down my throat when I studied the early

"Native" American stories in my college literature classes? Why don't they get this? Isn't this something that any rational thinking *progressive* teacher should acknowledge? And I want national standards to be compared to world norms. I don't want to know how our kids compare with those in Arkansas. I want to know how well our nation compares to other nations.

But it is important also that we provide the kids opportunities to fail and struggle as well as succeed and self reflect. I openly welcome the acknowledgement of other religions and cultures around the world, but I want all immigrants to assimilate into our American culture, like most of the early immigrants did. It's supposed to be a melting pot, but nobody's melting. Without forgetting from where we came, we were supposed to blend and develop a new culture and share a new heritage. They are using their heritage as a leveraging tool to cry "racist" and gain unearned "entitlements". So I remain a conservative.

So I am not sure this new school that I left Horizon Middle School for is moving the right way. Once again, I feel like I'm on an ice flow moving in the opposite direction of my heart. Certainly, this school promotes a different type of teaching that I need. But I was accomplishing that at every other school I taught at, if for no other reason than I learned how to unleash myself. It will be tough for a conservative like me to thrive in a school like this. Certain basic concerns eat away at me, like not disciplining kids because it might make them hate school even more. (Not thinking that it makes *me* or the *good* kids hate school even more when they are *not* disciplined.)

It's bizarre that at this school that I thought was going to provide me with a little more freedom, that I feel like I have actually been thrown into a fortress with a shorter, heavier leash. I feel like I'm in a chess game; I'm contemplating my next move. I'm trying to draw on some role models for help in these things, but all the good ones I know are either dead or fictional, or both. Either way they are inaccessible. I am rather finding a need to sit down and speak directly with one. Actually I thought Hamlet to be a very cunning problem solver, and Richard III was okay to watch at first but he was too much of a villain. All the tragedies seem to have these brilliant characters, but most of them end up in a stack of bodies. The comedies don't lend themselves well for character emulation because although they can put a couple of thoughts together to create a plan, they don't seem to make the great changes that I aspire to. Plus they all forgive each other at the end and next thing you know, all's well that ends well. Which is great, but Mr. Powell is still stuck out there in the ether not sure what to do next.

I think I've read every self-help book on the market to find out what to do next. There is such a volume of them now that they are repeating the themes of all the oldies. It's like music: all the good stuff has been written. All the decent sounding chord progressions have been around for years. Every once in awhile a book comes along that looks good though. But this is why Shakespeare is like a blue chip go-to-guy for me. His works are so full of truths, *just like math*. I believe the principles out there that are really something to scream about have been lurking around for thousands of years. The answers are out there, but not always readily noticeable. Just like our galaxy. From your back porch, it looks like hopelessly random smears of star dust. A closer, more poetic look might reveal the luster of the backbone of mother night. It's difficult to see the truths when we're too close to them. So what does our galaxy reveal to us when we look at it in "the big picture", perhaps from outside the galaxy itself? It is a beautifully organized system of spiraled matter that indicates intelligence and grand design. (This Chaos Theory fascinates me.)

So here I am sitting at crossroads, looking back from where I came, full of human truths sharpened by Shakespeare and some early Americans, purely fascinated by math, and smarter than I act. Steve, my brother-in-law says it best: nobody plays dumb like Dan. I have absolutely no idea how I am going to make it in teaching. I am much too animated for the old ways, and all the *progressive* teachers think I'll fall for anything.

I thought about dropping out of this insane nightmare and becoming a Shakespearean, but you know, if you know anything about the world of actors then you know we're talking about people connected to a completely different world. Mainly, themselves. My wife said it best, even though she is a performer. She describes many of them as so inner directed and self-serving that the concept of having children or "giving away" of themselves in this way without expecting something in return is much too alien. Oh sure, I know some of them have kids. It just simply seems this way with most of them.

What can I say? I'm an artist at heart myself. I don't know what the hurly burly is though, maybe getting away from throwing my life in the wind teaching school is something I need to get away from, although I won't. Maybe being around selfish and self-centered actors isn't any different than being around pre- and mid-pubescent middle schoolers. Most actors I've been around are socialists too, which is strange when you think how self-oriented they are.

My friend Marilyn the Librarian from a former school was always wondering why I didn't go teach Shakespeare classes at some of our local colleges. I don't want to teach it. I want to *do* it. So I stand out in the halls between classes and rev up my iambic pentameter and blank verse. I'm not sure I want to teach *anything.* I am inspired by those who find their passion and pursue it to the end of the earth. And I would much rather do than teach.

Teaching is doing something, I suppose, but I'd rather do something else. School teaching has become a high stakes concern. Standardized test scores and the numbers and statistics therein are all that matter to the state superintendents these days. They don't need a jack ass like me bouncing around the halls between classes with a stupid puppet on the end of his hand, and a sophomoric tool belt swinging wide in the doorways. They want ten percent increases every year in the test scores, not a breathing cartoon showing kids how a banana can be split lengthways into perfect thirds, or having them shout "Long live the king!" to the entire class before I do them a favor.

I actually went to one of our local community colleges recently and did some career testing. I decided to take several different tests that reveal different dimensions about my interests, abilities, skills and desires. I told them right up front not to recommend that I go into education because I would grab someone by the collar and head butt them if they did. This was about the time that the parent mafia was warming up their Volkswagen buses at this crazy place I was at. The process went on for a couple months with a test here and a discussion there. The lady was actually very friendly and knowledgeable but I really didn't find out anything about myself that I didn't already know.

It appeared that I was interested in the arts mostly, applied or spoken arts. No surprises there. I also let myself be assessed to see what career people I appeared to have similar interests with. Who were my interests most similar to? A technical writer of all things. My wife's Uncle Bob is a technical writer, and I enjoy his company tremendously. But I don't see myself stuck in front of a computer all the day long writing instructions to put together tricycles or how to program a graphing calculator. I have a hard enough time using my e-mail at work. Sometimes these technical manuals are successful at getting you to chase your own tail around for awhile. It's like they have to cater to the stupid people and in the process bring down everybody to the most inept level they could possibly perform at. Hey! It sounds just like public school teaching!

Some other things came up, librarian, advertising manager, corporate trainer and I think a forester. None of these had the power to move me. Oh yeah, radio broadcaster popped up there too. Being a corporate trainer sounded interesting but I don't think they would be a bit willing to let me saunter in to work with my tool belt hanging off my hips. Something about not wanting the clients to see this or something I presume. Sort of makes you wonder how I got away with it as long as I have.

One of the members of PC Administravia Politburo could've claimed it was an affront to construction workers in Mexico or something. I know the construction types could give a rip about my tool belt though. They think I'm one of their fraternity members. I was standing out in the hall one day taking a break from one of my mouthy classes and this district maintenance worker scurries up to me and tells me not to worry, that the roofing felt had arrived and it would be delivered to the east side of the school. I don't know why my shirt and tie didn't give him a least a sliver of a clue. Taking a closer look at some of the contents of my bag would've been some help too. I finally told him that I was in a different kind of construction business, that I help build other things. I've grown so accustomed to my tool belt that I don't believe I can think very well without it on, sort of like Sampson's hair and his strength. So I tend to wear it in front of everyone. I'm afraid I'll be rendered slobbering stupid and otherwise dull if I don't.

After dealing with some of these corrosive eighth graders, it's a wonder that I don't do autopsies for a living. I knew a guy when I went through graduate school to become a teacher who used to do autopsies and decided that he wanted to work with living people for a change and teach science. I bet it didn't take him too long to get back to the cadavers. Don't get me wrong, I claim that middle school kids are the best to be around. They know a little something so you don't have to wipe their noses at every turn, but when they get off the rails, oh they can be acrid, even more so around wimpy adults. In fact, I was inspired by these darlings to compile my own list of "All I Need to Know About Life I Learned From Eighth Graders":

~If it can't be understood, it's stupid and useless anyway.

~When people are even slightly different, they're retards.

~If a teacher, through some anomalous and unlikely event, discovers that you are indeed not behaving the way you claim to always behave, and purposes to point this out to you in class, pretend that you're not listening and by all means, don't look at him. This will scientifically and emphatically prove that you are, and always will be correct.

~When a teacher tries to correct your behavior, pretend you don't hear him. This releases you from any wrongdoing. However, if it's a peer that's trying to correct your behavior then it is perfectly okay to physically assault him. This still releases you from any wrongdoing.

~When adults try to correct your behavior and they are persistent enough to get your attention after three days of you pretending that you don't hear them, enough time has passed that you can easily deny that it ever happened in the first place. This releases you from any responsibility.

~People that work harder than you are simply lucky faggot retard preppies.

~When caught red-handed in front of any abiding adult, including God, and an immense body of other evidence that consequently pins the negative and unwanted truth on you, again simply deny that it ever happened. This Constitutionally releases you from any responsibility or even remote connection or association with such behavior now and in the future.

~The fact that you are sent to meet consequences proves the system doesn't work. You are then hereupon charged with being the object of compassion by suffering the throbs of martyrdom and injustice.

~If you don't like something such as consequences, it's not really happening to you. It is an evil, misfortunate, hallucinogenic, and gay stroke of policy of the conservative agenda.

~When facing accusations for a misdeed always lie, steal, cheat, deny, evade, and resist your way out of it. Defense lawyers always do this, therefore it *must* be moral.

But of course, these precepts only apply to a small number of the kids. It's the tail wagging the dog like everything else in society. I have actually defended middle school kids when I find myself overhearing conversations in the locker room about "kids these days". I said that there are *amazing* kids out there who are accomplishing tremendous things and demonstrating character beyond their years.

For example, many years ago I was putting some money in a pop machine for an after school refreshment. It was a typical and serene after school scene in the student foyer with scores of students running around and waiting for a bus, shouting the f-word and kicking each other in the balls. Why I couldn't wait to get to the staff room to do this I can't remember. But the machine took my money without producing my drink and I poked around a bit, shrugged my shoulders and walked off. Two minutes later this kid named Chris tapped me on the shoulder and said, "Here, Mr. Powell. I saw you trying to get a pop a minute ago and nothing came out. I think this is yours." He handed me my coins and took off.

I made it a point to thank him the next day when I caught up to him and made a bigger point to him that he had done something remarkable. I hope he is working with the youth of today, because I'm not sure I can do it. Most kids would've taken the change and then taken flight.

I will no doubt return to my most effective thinking practice to find my solutions: Alone at home, I sit at the piano, stare out the window and play. I suppose it's like smoking cigarettes for some people in that it's relaxing, and I personally find it thought provoking. It is sensible to expect that life is packed with conflict, apprehension, vagueness and contradiction. I'm not sure for all the creative solutions I can generate and all the possibilities of forming what I think are the best paths for others to follow that I am the right guy to have in a school. But there must be others who share my insane vision of bringing profound knowledge to kids so they can raise their own standards, change their limiting beliefs, and find strategies to improve their lives. And to do this without over-analyzing, short-sighted adults getting in the way, is simply asking too much.

It's just that I am only one man, and I seem to be thoroughly neural here at the crossroads. It will be interesting for me to get on my backward bicycle five years from now and turn around to see what decisions have emerged from me, in my time, the one man.

About the Author

Dan Powell sings Shakespearean sonnets. He and his sock puppet Bucky perform Shakespearean soliloquies. Dan wears a tool belt at work, and he can make thirteen year-olds laugh so hard they may even forget they live in poverty.

Dan Powell has also committed some serious and embarrassing mistakes in his life, and has fought his way out of deep debt. He knows that people actually need failure to grow.

He is independent in spirit, like 1776, like the air that passes over the planet, or like wild mustangs that run across the plains. A marine once taught him to adapt, modify, overcome, and improvise, but he still can't always.

He has been called gifted, and he has been called a jack of all asses.

Dan sometimes dresses like an insurance salesman, and is much smarter than the kid he acts like. He has a wife out of a fairy tale who once called him a folk hero, an entrepreneurial daughter, and a son who will someday beat him in full contact chess.

And, for what it's worth, Dan Powell is also a middle school math teacher.

Made in the USA
Las Vegas, NV
15 February 2022

43962073R00105